IN THE LIGHT OF DEATH

IN THE LIGHT OF DEATH

Experiences on the Threshold Between Life and Death

by

INEKE KOEDAM

www.whitecrowbooks.com

CONTENTS

PREFACE

This thought-provoking and fascinating book discusses the intense process of dying, the process of acceptance and surrender, and in particular the extraordinary experiences that apparently occur quite often during the dying process. It's such a significant story because, to this day in Western society, dying and death are still considered taboo subjects. Death is a concept that has seemingly been banished from our society, although 'death' itself is perfectly natural; people die every day. In the Netherlands for instance, an average of 375 people die each day, meaning that approximately 135,000 people die every year. Dying is as natural as being born. The questions we ask most in the final stages of our lives are: what does death really mean, what is life, and what will happen after I die? Why are most people so afraid of it? Can't death also be seen as a welcome release after the sufferings of unrelenting illness? Why do doctors often still experience a patient's death as a failure because the patient didn't stay alive? Why aren't people today, in the final stages of their life, allowed to 'simply' die following a serious, incurable illness, instead of choosing to go through chemotherapy or being kept alive by a respirator or fed artificially through tubes? Why is our initial reaction to hang on to life and to put off the moment of death no matter what? A doctor's priority is usually to keep a patient alive as long as possible, usually in accordance with the patient's wishes, who in spite of the debilitations, pain and anxiety still wants to stay alive as long as possible. This is why we often hear about ongoing treatment or overtreatment. Is our fear of death the main cause of this and does this fear stem from the fact that we don't really know what death is? Without passing any kind of judgement, one can imagine that, as long as the patient and his or her family focus on the treatment, the inner preparation for death is neglected. When it eventually becomes clear that there really is no point in further treatment, it is then said that 'the patient is beyond treatment', that 'nothing more can be done for the patient', and these incurably ill patients are then often referred onward to a hospice. In hospices, it is accepted and expected that people will pass away and it is here that the taboo about death can be overcome. This is of course an intense process, for the patients and their families, as well as for those who work in terminal and palliative care.

In contrast to hospice caregivers, death is a taboo subject for most terminally ill patients and their families, because they've tried to deny or postpone the end of life and their own process of dying for as long as they can. And so they suppress all thoughts about the finality of life and avoid talking about it. It's only natural that dying and having to say goodbye evokes all kinds of emotions. Some cherish the idea of finding reconciliation in their life, by coming to terms with the life they lived or being able to say goodbye to their loved ones. Others prefer to go to bed one night and simply not wake up again the next day. There are also those who wish to die a painless death, who would like to stay in control or die in a dignified manner. As with all phases of our lives, dying is much less of a manageable or controllable process than we would like it to be. Time and time again we are faced with the fact that, in most cases, the circumstances of our deaths will be completely out of our control. We become fearful and unsure at the prospect of having to say goodbye to loved ones and many of us have no idea how to deal with the emotions and feelings we will face.

Our own unresolved emotional issues also play a role when someone near to us is facing death. We lose our capacity to say and do those things we intuitively know are right. Despair and isolation could be the consequence, and not just for the person facing death. Family and friends also suffer when they aren't able to understand what is happening. The person who is dying usually knows deep down that he or she is in the final stages of life. Families are also often aware that the end is near, yet they generally don't dare to speak openly about it. In a hospice, it's important and a great challenge to make terminal patients ('residents') aware of what they already know, albeit subconsciously.

In this book, Ineke Koedam consciously devotes specific attention to the extraordinary experiences of awareness that can occur during the final stages of life, because they seem to foretell the impending death, and can offer comfort during the dying process, for the patient, the family, as well as the hospice caregivers.

We regularly hear of special experiences, such as deathbed visions, from people who are close to dying. Family members and hospice caregivers have come across these experiences but are often reluctant to talk about them out of fear of not being believed. We only begin to realise the significance of these experiences and the deep impression they leave the moment people have the courage to talk openly to others about them. The most common phenomena, or at least those that are reported the most, are the so-called visions that are experienced during the final stages before death. A well-known example of a deathbed vision is that in the days or weeks before his or her death, a patient will talk about visitations from a deceased partner or from parents, children, family members, friends and sometimes even religious figures. Patients report that these people who have already died have come to collect them or to help them to release themselves from their bodily illnesses and their life. The fact that one can contact the conscious soul of deceased loved ones and communicate with them, provides an entirely new perspective on what death could be like. What it seems to suggest is that those who are dying are met by loved ones who have already passed on and are taken to another non-earthly reality full of light, peace and unimaginable love; a reality that is usually considered much more real than our own daily lives. It's as though the dying can move between different 'worlds'. Sometimes they say that they have been somewhere else, but this is also noticed by families and hospice caregivers. In most cases, these events are seen as spiritual experiences which alleviate the dying process and ease the transition into death. Experiences of the dying make us aware of the possibility that there is life after death. These experiences often seem to help the dying let go of the physical world and overcome their fear of death, and indeed can sometimes offer comfort to those who are left behind, if the experiences are understood and accepted. Many of the reports of deathbed visions or end-of-life experiences are not seen as such, or are interpreted as hallucinations, terminal confusion, or the side-effects of medication. However, these deathbed experiences simply cannot be compared with the hallucinations that result from medication, confusion, or dementia, which cause fear and anxiety. End-of-life experiences usually occur during a state of clear consciousness and seem to be powerful personal experiences which are hugely significant for those involved, as well as for their families, friends and carers. When people are nearing the end of their lives, they take stock of the lives they have lived. This can kindle a desire for reconcilement and prompt the person dying to resolve unfinished business in life before death. Settling unfinished issues alleviates existential unrest and discomfort and enables the dying soul to prepare spiritually for approaching death. Reconcilement doesn't just concern relationships with family members and loved ones; it is also about acceptance of the life lived. When it comes to the final reckoning, it is always the dying person who passes final judgement, and this is when believers need God's mercy. By coming to terms with life as it was lived, the dying person can better prepare for approaching death. End-of-life experiences seem to play a vital role in this process.

Those who have never dealt with end-of-life experiences described in this book might easily dismiss them as fantasy or as some kind of disorientation or confusion. But when people have gone through such an experience themselves, it leaves behind a deep and lasting impression. It will often lead them to see death from a different perspective. Many will gain new insights into what dying really means and will find profound meaning in both life and death. End-of-life experiences are usually comforting, encouraging, and reassuring for the dying and for close family members. Hospice caregivers often recognise what is happening and call such experiences meaningful, valuable and profound. The experience we call death is a process that belongs solely to the person dying and the question remains whether carers and family members are willing to grant him or her this unique and essential process. It not only asks for an open attitude from those who are close but also an understanding of what dying really is so we can truly allow the dying to deal with the process themselves and not unnecessarily interfere in our own interpretations of what is right. End-of-life experiences transcend thought and judgement. Each person dies in his or her own way. That's not to say that people die as they have lived. Dying is the last chapter of our lives and is unique for each and every one of us. There simply is no wrong or right way.

In respect of both content and consequences, end-of-life experiences can be identical to near-death experiences, which can be explained by the notion that consciousness can function outside the body independent of brain activity. The concept of this boundless consciousness, not withheld by time or space, can explain not only end-of-life experiences but also other phenomena connected with death, such as the appearance of one's parents at the moment of death, known as a perimortal experience. This kind of experience often takes place at night. It isn't really a dream but rather a kind of conscious contact while we are asleep, which leaves a particularly deep impression and has a much greater feeling of reality than an ordinary dream. With perimortal experiences we receive, sometimes from a great distance, information about the moment of death and sometimes even the way in which the loved one has died, even though we could not possibly have known these details when they actually happened.

In this context, it is also interesting to mention terminal lucidity, where patients who have suffered from Alzheimer's disease or severe dementia for years and who no longer recognize their families, suddenly have a moment of lucidity in the last moments of their lives and are able to recognise their children or partners and call them by name, say goodbye, after which they can pass on. This terminal lucidity has also been reported in patients who for days have been unable to talk or who are in a coma. These experiences cannot be explained by our current medical knowledge, because the brains of these terminal patients are seriously damaged. However, a considerable number of nursing staff in hospices are quite aware of this terminal lucidity affecting dying patients.

A shared death experience, also called an empathic near-death experience (NDE), is experienced by healthy people who are present at a deathbed, when at the very moment of death their consciousness is absorbed into the death experience of the loved one. They leave their bodies and travel through the tunnel towards the light. They will sometimes see family members who have passed on and even the flashbacks of the life of the loved one who has just died. Then they suddenly return to their own bodies to stand once again at the bedside of their loved one. Raymond Moody has recently written a book about these kinds of experiences, in which he points out that these experiences can be identical to an NDE but they affect completely healthy people who have a close bond with the dying person.

Since nursing staff and volunteers, particularly those working in hospices and other terminal care facilities, are more open to all these special experiences that can occur with dying patients, they are recognised and acknowledged more often. Dying patients should be given the room to talk about them, without carers or family members casting doubts about what they have experienced. When nursing staff ask open-ended questions about these kinds of experiences, it becomes a great source of support for both the patient and the family, because an end-of-life experience can considerably lessen the fear of impending death for patients and families. By being open to the significance of the content and the consequences of this broadened or heightened awareness in the last stages of life, it is possible for the terminal patient, their family, and the hospice caregivers to gain new understanding into the nature of death, which is simply the end of our physical being, while our essence, our conscious self will still exist.

It has become apparent from the special study carried out by Ineke Koedam amongst staff in several hospices in the Netherlands that end-of-life experiences are more common than we might think and that they happen in the weeks, days or hours before death. All workers in the healthcare sector, as well as dying patients and their families, should be made aware of the special experiences which can occur in the final stages of death. Significant life changes, including the disappearance of the fear of death, are often the results of these experiences. By giving these experiences scope and attention, without passing any kind of judgement or opinion, the patient and their family can integrate the experience into whatever remains of that life. It is therefore crucial to concentrate on the individual expressions and needs of the dying and to listen to and accept their end-of-life experiences without judgement or commentary. The recognition and acceptance of the experiences and feelings of the dying during the transition into death, such as the end-of-life experiences described in this book, are actually part of spiritual care. In the definition of palliative care, it states that not only physical care but also mental, social and spiritual care are vital. We must try to avoid interjecting our own beliefs and assumptions about dying and death. I am convinced that this book will make a huge contribution to the acknowledgement and recognition of end-of-life experiences, which can diminish the fear of death even in its final stages.

Pim van Lommel, Cardiologist,
author of *Consciousness Beyond Life:
The Science of Near-Death Experience.*

INTRODUCTION

Why did I write this book about experiences and phenomena on the threshold between life and death? From the end of 2009 until the middle of 2011, I carried out a small-scale study into deathbed phenomena in the Netherlands on behalf of the prominent English neuropsychiatrist Peter Fenwick. The results of his research in England give reason to regard death as a process rather than a single event. Death is often heralded by phenomena, such as visions or coincidences. For quite some time, I myself was involved with Hospice De Vier Vogels (The Fours Birds) in Rotterdam, first as a volunteer and later as coordinator, so for me this was nothing new. My first personal experience in this regard went back to when I was thirteen years old. Grandma, on my father's side, had died. Although my sisters and I were allowed a quick look inside the coffin, we were mostly kept far from what was the first death in our lives. As far as I can remember, I didn't specifically have a closer connection with my grandmother than my sisters did. However, that evening, my grandma chose to visit me and sat at the foot of my bed. Many years later while I was working as a volunteer in the hospice, she honoured me with another visitation, this time in a meaningful dream.

In 2009, I assisted with a symposium 'Endless Consciousness' about near-death experiences, deathbed phenomena and visions. Pim van Lommel and Peter Fenwick were the preeminent speakers. The research carried out by both scientists demonstrates that there is good reason to assume that our consciousness does not always converge with our brain functions. How would it be if consciousness does not end when the body dies? What would happen if humanity was to discover that death is not an ending but rather a *transition*? How can we find out what happens during this transition? How can we stay near one other at the hour of death? An in-depth understanding of the states of consciousness and of the apperceptions of those dying can help us to explore these questions.

The more than interested audience encouraged Fenwick to pursue his research in the Netherlands and some days later we visited the hospice in Rotterdam together. Fenwick is deeply impressed by this hospice and uses De Vier Vogels as model in his readings at conferences and symposia all over the world. It seems obvious that I should carry on his research in the Netherlands, and that is indeed what is happening. I have found three hospices prepared to work with me doing this research: the Kajan Hospice in Hilversum, the Johannes Hospitium De Ronde Venen in Wilnis and the hospice to which I am already attached to, De Vier Vogels in Rotterdam. In my study, I am joined by a total of twenty-one volunteers, five nurses, a complementary care nurse, a music therapist, and two supervisors.

Back then I had no intention at all of writing a book about these experiences. It was only at the beginning of 2012 that the idea arose of letting hospice caregivers have their say, having heard from the scientists, I decided to put this precious material together in a book. No scientific statistics, but real experiences and observations of hospice staff who work on the boundary between life and death. We can learn so much from them when it comes to observations and experiences of those who are dying. I look back at those truly genuine meetings with those who took part in the study with immense gratitude. It's therefore especially important for me to keep their experiences 'undiluted'. It isn't about whether they are right or wrong, true or untrue. After all, they are activities of the mind and these experiences transcend our mental capacities. Many have had special experiences surrounding death but have never dared to speak out before now. Occasionally, they keep them to themselves like precious gems, but more commonly because they are afraid of not being taken seriously. Perhaps they will find some encouragement and empowerment in reading about the experiences of others.

I invite you, dear reader, to read this book with an open heart and to realise how precious and sometimes fragile these experiences can be for those involved. The three hospices and those who took part in the study have been generous in their support for the plan to write this book, because they sincerely hope that their knowledge, wisdom, and experience will make a contribution to the care for the dying. Not just in hospices, where the awareness of death and dying is relatively high, but also in other institutions and hospitals.

It is most definitely not my intention to romanticise death or the care of the dying. You can read more about this in my conclusion. No one knows why one person and not the other experience these kinds of phenomena. It certainly isn't a benchmark for a good transition. But in my experience, recognising and accepting these deathbed phenomena when they do occur most surely is.

In this book I first look briefly back at past research carried out into deathbed phenomena, with my thanks to Fenwick. Then I examine the studies carried out by Fenwick in England and the Netherlands, after which I discuss the various experiences and phenomena, the distinction Fenwick makes between transpersonal and final meaning experiences, and how these experiences differ from hallucinations caused by medication, confusion, and dementia.

We then hear from the hospice caregivers themselves. Their contributions have been abridged and edited, without compromising the content or the individuality of those interviewed. Their names are used throughout. However, the names of the deceased are fictitious out of respect. The following chapter covers experiences during after death care, the care which takes place shortly after death. Next, we examine the specific role of hospice caregivers, together with the effects these experiences have on the dying, their family and friends as well as the carers. It's not only deathbed phenomena that announce that death is near. There are other indicators that seem to show that the person dying is preparing for the final end. We discuss that process, as well as the physical aspects of dying, in the chapter *Dealing with death*. And finally, how can we be open to what happens during the transition and what can we learn from the hospice caregivers in this respect? The final chapter examines the various aspects of communication and the importance of spiritual care.

Dying is a precious and essential process of each and every person, and it is my hope that this book will provide support during this process. I also hope that it will help to broaden awareness of the transition period during death. Are you personally involved in the process of dying, perhaps as a caregiver, professionally, or as a volunteer? Are you an expert or simply interested? This book paints a picture of how the dying prepare themselves and how profound meaning can be found in the process of dying.

DEATH AS A MYSTERY

——————>●<——————

Death has always been surrounded by mystery and by symbols, ritual, and traditions in every culture. Eastern tradition has always maintained a rich culture concerning the passage through death and the life thereafter. The Middle Ages too were steeped in the art of dying. The Christianity of the Dark Ages fully embraced the art of dying, the so-called *Ars Moriendi*; a desire to leave this life completely, reconciled with God, and to be an example to others on one's deathbed. In western society, historically speaking, death and its accompanying phenomena and experiences connected with death are rooted in Christian beliefs. It was mainly progress in science in the nineteenth century that put an end to this in the West.

One of the most famous illustrations of deathbed phenomena can be found in Giotto's frescos in the Church of Saint Francis. The dying Saint Francis of Assisi is depicted surrounded by angels, while another picture shows a dying monk in a different part of Italy. This monk is conscious of the dying Saint Francis and calls out to him: 'Wait for me Saint Francis, I am coming, I am coming!'

Regardless of our personal beliefs or spiritual convictions, none of us can really be certain of what happens after death. Even so, we know that deathbed phenomena have been experienced for thousands of years and have been recognised in many different cultures and spiritual traditions. Within (medical) scientific circles, there is an ever increasing acceptance that these experiences are more than simply deathbed visions, which is how they have usually been reported, and that they are not at all uncommon. It is primarily thanks to research conducted by

1

scientists such as Raymond Moody (America), Pim van Lommel (the Netherlands) and Peter Fenwick (Great Britain), that there is now also an increasing willingness in the West to look closely at the subject of death from a wider viewpoint.

HISTORY

—————➤●◄—————

In the book *The Art of Dying* by Peter and Elizabeth Fenwick, we learn that phenomena such as apparitions and ghosts were first taken seriously in the seventeenth century. Around the turn of the nineteenth century, a distinction was made between the various forms of apparitions. If a deceased person appeared to someone who was well and healthy, it was usually in order to pass on information to that person. However, if the apparition appeared to someone who was dying, it was not only to announce that death was approaching but also to help them through the coming experience. The first study into this took place at the end of the nineteenth century by the medical researchers Gurney, Myers, and Podmore. Their book entitled *Phantasms of the Living* was first published in 1886 and contained a fascinating collection of uncommon experiences.

The first scientific study was undertaken in 1920 by Sir William Barrett, medical professor at the Royal College of Science in Dublin. His interest was ignited after his wife, who was a midwife, had such an experience herself. Lady Barrett was asked to help a woman called Doris, who was in direst need. Her baby was delivered safely, but Doris died after giving birth. Lady Barrett tells how Doris started to have visions: "Suddenly she looked eagerly towards one particular corner of the room, a radiant smile illuminating her whole countenance. 'Oh, lovely, lovely', cried Doris." When asked what it was she saw, Doris answered: 'Lovely brightness, wonderful beings.' A moment later she called out: 'Oh, Father, he's so happy that I'm coming, he's so happy. If only William could come too.'

Doris spoke to her father again and told him that she was coming, and told Lady Barrett: 'Oh, he's so close.' Then she seemed confused: 'He has Vida with him, Vida is with him.' It was this last remark that convinced Sir William that this was a genuine experience. Vida was Doris's sister, to whom she was very close. Vida had in fact died shortly before but because of Doris's serious condition, she had not been told. The fact that she had seen her sister with her deceased father, while she thought that Vida was alive and well, convinced Sir William. He could no longer dismiss the incident as insignificant. This event made such a deep impression that he himself began to have similar experiences and recorded them in his book *Deathbed Visions* (1926). He concluded that this kind of experience was not just the by-product of the brain shutting down, but could also happen to people who were still conscious and in full possession of their wits.

The first comprehensive and objective study was carried out by Karlis Osis and Erlendur Haraldsson. Initially, in 1961, Osis researched hallucinations experienced by terminally ill patients by means of a questionnaire given to 5,000 doctors and 5,000 nursing staff. After analysing the results, Osis identified two types of hallucinations: firstly visions of nature and landscapes in which no people were present, and secondly, the appearance of deceased relatives and friends who come to help the dying pass over to the next life. Then Osis, together with Haraldsson, extended the research by conducting two comprehensive follow-up studies in the United States (1961) and India (1972). The results were remarkable. The research in the United States revealed that most apparitions involved deceased loved ones, while religious companions seldom appeared. The research in India had the opposite results: there, the companions and messengers were mostly religious figures, while the appearance of loved ones was rarely reported. This clearly shows that whatever the meaning or purpose of such experiences might be, they definitely contain a certain cultural element. This is confirmed by the fact that, due to the changing viewpoints on death in the West from the nineteenth century onwards, deathbed visitations involved deceased family and friends decidedly more often than religious figures such as Christ or the Virgin Mary.

PETER FENWICK'S RESEARCH

Dr Peter Fenwick, Senior Lecturer Emeritus of Neuropsychiatry in London, is an authority in the field of near-death experiences. Fenwick's interest in near-death experiences was sparked after reading Raymond Moody's book *Life After Life*. Initially sceptical, he changed his mind after a conversation with one of his patients who described his own near-death experience, which bore many similarities to those described by Moody. Thereafter, Fenwick also attracted publicity following his research into so-called 'end-of-life experiences', the phenomena and experiences which seem to herald approaching death. Together with Sue Brayne and Hilary Lovelace, he looked into the implications of these experiences on palliative care.

The outcome of his study into near-death experiences reported by patients in coronary care units after having a heart attack, was that about ten percent of people who recovered had had a near-death experience. This percentage corresponds to what other researchers such as Van Lommel had determined earlier. These near-death experiences, probably more aptly called 'actual death experiences', since these patients were actually clinically dead, have the same characteristics as the experiences studied by Fenwick, which announce that death is imminent, such as going into the light, experiencing a different reality and meeting deceased loved ones who have come to offer support, reassurance, to collect them or indeed to send them back. However, the deepest impressions they leave are feelings of peace, intense compassion, and love and light. Those who have had a near-death experience are absolutely convinced that if they had gone with their loved ones, they would have died. These are profound experiences which have had huge and lasting impacts on their lives.

> She suddenly looked up towards the window and seemed to be staring intensely at something. Then she turned to me and said: 'Pauline, don't ever be afraid of dying. I have seen a beautiful light and was going towards it ... it was so peaceful, and I really had to fight to come back.' The next day when I wanted to go home, I said: 'Bye Mum, see you tomorrow.' She looked me straight in the eye and replied: 'I'm not worried about tomorrow and you mustn't be either, promise me.' She died the next day. I was sad, but at the same time I knew she had seen something that gave her comfort and peace when she knew she was going to die.

It was this experience of one of his patients that intrigued Fenwick and set him on the path of further study. After all, it had so many of the characteristics of a near-death experience. Firstly, seeing the light, the feeling of peace, and the fact that Pauline's mother found it so difficult to return after catching a glimpse of another reality, plus the absence of any fear of the approaching death. Secondly, it seemed clear that Pauline's mother knew that she was about to die. Fenwick thought that perhaps we should not see such experiences as isolated events which happen at that moment when life is about to be snuffed out, but rather as part of a continuation, of a process, the process of dying. They seem to represent a kind of preparation. A preparation that begins hours or even days before death.

After an extensive interview in a Scottish newspaper and his appearance on English national television, Fenwick was inundated with reactions from all over the country. This mass response made it clear that deathbed phenomena were much more common than previously thought, but above all that they were enormously varied. The following experience was particularly convincing, which took place many years ago and made a deep impression on the man who recounted what happened.

> In 1950, a distant family relative, John, was in hospital in Inverness. It was a Sunday and my father had gone to the hospital to visit him.

When he arrived, he was told that John had died that morning. The hospital asked my father to inform the next of kin, his sister Kate and her husband, that John had died. They were sheep farmers living on a remote farm in Easter Ross and had no telephone. My father and I drove to the farm. When we arrived, Kate said 'I know why you've come, I heard him calling me, "Kate, Kate", when he died.' She said this in a very matter of fact way and told us what time he had died, which corresponded exactly with the time of death recorded by the hospital. I found this an amazing experience which I have never forgotten, nor will I ever. I was seventeen years old at the time.

This is a beautiful example of another phenomenon, the deathbed coincidence. This is just one of a series of experiences and phenomena which can take place during the dying process. For a person who has never had such an experience, it can be very difficult to accept it as the truth. Yet it is not uncommon to sense the strongest of feelings that someone close to you has died. This is also what Christina told me about what happened around the time her father died. Not only did she already know her father had died when she received the news, she also experienced a special farewell and could feel what her father went through at the moment he died. Christina, who comes from Brazil, was living in America when her father died. She's now been living in the Netherlands for 21 years. When Christina tells me her story, it is obvious what a deep impression it made on her.

It all happened on a beautiful day. I woke up and the sky was blue. I was studying at the Manhattanville College in New York State. It was a weekday, I can't remember exactly what day but I know I had a lecture to go to. I was nineteen years old. My father called me on the telephone, I think it was around 12 o'clock. With the time difference, it was about 8 o'clock for him in Brazil. He was just calling to say hello and sounded perfectly normal. I didn't notice anything odd in his voice. It was just a short phone call, nothing out of the ordinary. Then I had to go to my lecture as usual, but on that particular day I suddenly felt strange, very sad and withdrawn. I thought: I really don't feel well, and decided not to go to my lecture after all. At the time I would often spend time writing poetry. So I grabbed my notebook and a pen and went to campus. There was a beautiful meadow there with trees and I went to sit under one of the trees. I would often write poems without really having to think; they just seemed to come to me. When I had finished, I read what I'd written down and thought: oh, so that's what it means. That afternoon, I'd written a long poem about the sea, about the ebb and flow. Just like life, it comes and it goes. Coming and going, coming and going.

I don't remember much about the rest of that day. It felt like such a strange, empty day. But I remember the morning when I was sitting under the tree quite clearly, and that evening when I got a phone call; it was 7 o'clock. It was my aunt and all she said was: 'Christina.' I replied: 'My father's dead.' So strange. The words just came out of my mouth. I needed to go home as soon as I could and get things sorted out, but I couldn't leave until the following day. That evening, just before going to bed, I put on some music, lovely instrumental piano music. I was listening to it and swaying ever so slightly to the rhythm. Yes... it was as though I could feel him. He held me tight, it was so strange, he hugged me, really hugged me ... as though he were saying goodbye. Then I went to bed and had the most beautiful dream. Above a meadow, just like the one where I had written the poem, there was a rainbow arcing across the blue sky. There was a camera around my neck. And God, or a voice, said to me: 'You can take a photo of the rainbow, but if you do you'll have an asthma attack, and if you don't take the photo you won't.' I took the photo of the rainbow and I woke up unable to breathe, or at least not without difficulty. I have no idea if I woke up at night or in the morning. Time felt strange. But this was how my father died, after an asthma attack and heart failure. I had felt what my father was going through at the time of his death.

I had experienced something very strange and special in a short space of time, especially that he came to dance with me for a while; at least that's want I want to believe. I had goose bumps all over, it was so extraordinary and I will never forget it. Nothing has ever made a deeper impression on me than what happened on that day.

I never saw my father again. When I arrived in Brazil, everything had been arranged and the funeral was all over. That's how it goes in Brazil, and I found that very hard. What was wonderful though, was when my mother told me that when my father died he was smiling. Then all is well, I thought. Yes, this brings some solace to your heart.

People are often reluctant to talk about these kinds of experiences because they are afraid that no one will believe them. When I see the effect that talking about it has on them, I realise how meaningful and profound these experiences are. It doesn't matter how long ago it was, talking about it is to relive the experience. The most common phenomena, or at least those most commonly reported, are the so-called visions, the coincidences and the observation that 'something' seems to leave the body at the moment of death. Later on, we will talk about the phenomena and sightings identified by Fenwick, followed by the experiences of hospice caregivers with these phenomena. Before that however, let us discuss the studies carried out in the Netherlands.

RESEARCH CARRIED OUT
IN THE NETHERLANDS

As Fenwick shows in his research, death can be regarded as a process rather than a single event, and it can be announced or heralded by unusual events, sightings or experiences; the so-called deathbed phenomena. These phenomena can offer comfort to the person dying and help him or her to prepare for the coming transition. Until the present day, very little research was ever conducted into these specific phenomena, the frequency and effect on family, friends and carers. Fenwick's research is intended to develop a deeper understanding of these phenomena in order to help nursing staff, volunteers, family, and friends to be able to experience the process of dying more consciously and so to provide the best support.

We can ensure a "good death" for ourselves and help those we love to achieve it too. *The Art of Dying* demonstrates that we can face death with a peaceful and untroubled mind; that death is not a lonely or fearful journey, but an intensely hopeful one', according to the back cover of *The Art of Dying*.

The studies carried out in the Netherlands took place between 2009 and 2011. Thirty hospice caregivers from three different hospices took part. Participation was of course entirely voluntary. Those who took part felt that it was a good, important, and meaningful study. It is also notable that the participants have an above average interest in consciousness and spirituality, and a high degree of involvement in the process of dying and everything around it. For most people, their desire to be involved was twofold. Firstly, they wanted to take part in the study so they could spread their understanding and knowledge of deathbed phenomena further and make these phenomena more accessible and acceptable to others. Secondly, to improve their own development and to allow them to support the dying process even better, or as one volunteer put it: 'To become more aware of myself and what I do'. Another said: 'I am very interested in everything to do with the deathbed. I am also searching for answers myself. I really hope that I will learn a lot. I believe this study is very important because there is just so much we don't know yet. We simply don't know what a person still goes through or hears.'

Simone, supervisor:

> In the first place, I find it worthwhile that the survey receives broader support and that the knowledge 'there is more' should spread further and wider into other, larger institutions. And also that more will be possible, resulting in a more all-round care. Secondly, it personally forces me to become more aware. Taking part has also made me more connected to the here and now. It helps me to continuously stay attuned. Thirdly, I feel it is a good incentive for the hospices to work together to stay in tune and to keep developing.

The study comprised two personal in-depth interviews. The first after the participant filled in a questionnaire that looks back at experiences and observations of the preceding five years. The second, one year later, after filling in a questionnaire about experiences and observations for that particular year. The Dutch results showed us that, although the participants were rather less steadfast in their answers on the second questionnaire, their viewpoints had not changed to any great degree. Taking part was helpful for some of the participants because it made them really think about the subject and helped them to be more alert and aware. Others found the study more inhibiting, because they found themselves thinking too much and therefore less open and present in the here and now. A few had doubts. Especially if no experiences had actually occurred in their presence, they would ask themselves: "Am I doing it right? Am I really good enough? What could I be doing wrong?" It was frustrating and difficult for these people to bring it out into the open. A fantastic achievement on their part.

I find it essential to emphasise once again that there really is no right or wrong way; there is just the experience, or the absence of one. That is what matters. Furthermore, it was apparent that there was an undivided, sincere willingness to provide the best possible support for the dying. Finally, I found that without exception everyone appreciated the opportunity to tell their story, to be able to talk about personal, precious and sometimes fragile experiences. I felt genuinely privileged to hear about them, especially when hospice caregivers themselves were part of the experience. You can read about such an experience below in an interview with one of the volunteers.

Jeannie:

> She was lying on her side and I sat in a chair by her side. She looked at me with her large blue eyes. She was a bit younger than me. I told her that her family were on their way and that everything was alright, that I would stay with her and that she was doing fine. I put my hand over hers and felt incredibly close to her. I didn't say much and we just looked at each other ... and we kept on looking. It was as though we were interlocked by this captivation through our eyes. It was so overwhelming and I became very still. I felt as though it lasted for a long time, but it can only have been for a moment. While we were looking at each other, she died. She died, of that I'm sure, but she was still looking at me. I will never forget that moment as long as I live. Everything was light, I was light. There was a blue light all around. I was there, and yet I wasn't. So much happened during that moment, everything lifted away. I felt as though ... oh, there just aren't any words. So I sat there and began to cry, still looking at her. Then the experience ebbed away and I thanked her.

In this book, every attention is given to the stories of the hospice caregivers, rather than to the data collected from the questionnaires. On the one hand, to know more about their experiences with these specific phenomena and, on the other hand, to learn from them about the care for the dying and making advancements in creating a wider perspective of these essential moments in human life.

PHENOMENA AND SIGHTINGS WHEN DEATH IS APPROACHING

During the final stages of our lives, we can observe to a greater or lesser degree a definite spiritualisation. The connection with the body is reduced, and the dividing line between our inner and outer selves becomes thinner and thinner. We know, not only from research, but also from daily practice at hospices that people who are facing death tend to feel the need to come to terms with their lives. Someone who is particularly aware will do this at an earlier stage, but most of us, if it is given to us, will want to come to terms with the lives we have lived, or lives that we may see as unfinished, as death approaches. Disappointments, failures, regrets about what we have done or have left undone, shortcomings. So much happens in our lives that we would like to come to terms with in order to have a peaceful transition. This desire to take stock and thus resolve unfinished business, especially with family, seems to be an autonomous aspect of the process of life. Perhaps it is inherent to the mysteries of life and death.

It is also not uncommon for someone who is dying, in the days or weeks before their death, to talk about visits from deceased relatives or friends, children, religious figures or even favourite pets. They say that these individuals have come to collect them, or to help them to let go of life. In one of the interviews, Nurse Wilma talks about a conversation she had with an elderly lady:

> She had a very orthodox Catholic background, and she always wanted us to get her out of bed at 6 every morning so she could sit in her chair by the window and say her prayers. She would pray for us, for the world. She prayed for everything that had happened. She had been with us for three or four months when she stopped wanting to do it as often. She didn't get out of bed as much, but she still wanted us to wake her in the morning. One day she said: 'Wilma, I'm not confused but I can see my husband.' I replied: 'Goodness, what does he look like?' She answered: 'The same as he always did. Can you imagine?' Me: 'Oh yes, is it a good feeling?' She: 'Yes, it's very good.' Me: 'What would you like to ask him? He's here and he wants to help you.' She: 'I am finding it hard to leave my two sons behind. They're both grown men but they don't get along and I so want things to be better between them. They also don't go to church anymore.' I said: 'I can see that this is really hard for you. What do you want to ask your husband?' Then she took my hand and asked her husband: 'Can Wilma stay?' I could. Then she said: 'I want to come with you but something's still worrying me. Our sons don't go to church anymore and they can't get on with each other. Can you do anything to help?' I said: 'It's wonderful that you ask him to help. You can pray, but perhaps your husband can do something in his own way too.'
>
> That very same week, both sons came to visit and told me they were unhappy with how things were between them. They asked me: 'Would you talk to us? Just with the two of us first, and then with Mother? We can notice that she's finding it difficult to let go because we aren't getting along with one another.' I told them that it was indeed very difficult for their mother and that she had had contact with their father. I said: 'I know you can't promise anything, but it's wonderful that you are sitting together now, that you have both had the same idea quite independently. It's quite possible that your father has sent you both a message.'

Within a week, the lady died very peacefully.

Those people who are nearing the end find it easy to transit to and from other realities and describe other worlds. They talk about going on a journey, suddenly stare at a particular point in the room or turn towards the window and express feelings of surprise, joy, or wonder.

Even those who are semiconscious and unable to communicate with their families, friends or carers will seem to reach out for something and grasp it, and then feel it with their fingers in puzzlement. Sometimes the dying seem to be deep in thought, as though they were processing information.

We don't know how many of the dying have visions or experiences like these. It's possible that many such experiences are simply not reported because the person dying is afraid of being seen as confused or fearful, and therefore scared of having to take medicine, against his or her will to stop it from happening again.

Volunteer Anke:

> At first she said: 'Don't you think it's crazy, it's just not possible'. She was very hesitant at first but she felt she could confide in me. She noticed that too.

> Anke explained that some people are very reluctant to talk about these phenomena. The question is, does this have to do with the person dying who is scared of appearing confused, or is it possibly something to do with the people around? Apparently this lady felt a receptive and non-judgemental person in Anke and, although hesitant, she talked about her experience. Could it be that people are so hesitant because they feel unable to share their stories? Anke: 'I think that both hold very true. When you talk about an experience like this, you're making yourself very vulnerable and you become incredibly dependant on the one who is listening, who receives the story.'

> I talked with nurse Loes about the fact that she had been working with the dying for some time, but that she had not come across any specific end-of-life experiences, unlike her close colleague. Could she explain this?

Loes:

> Maybe it has to do with how I get by in life. I'm a typical Dutch woman, practical in my ways. I have a religious background, but don't really practice it. It's not an important part of my life. I am always ready to respect my patients' choices, so I'm willing to accommodate them. If they want to hear something from the Bible, I'll read to them. But because I am not really receptive to end-of-life experiences, people

may not come to me so easily. I look at things in a very matter-of-fact way. I'm not spiritual. That kind of thing doesn't affect me and perhaps that's why they would rather confide in someone else. That doesn't mean I dismiss it though. The fact that it has no real significance for me, doesn't stop me from being there for the dying.

Nursing staff may not talk about it because they think they will come across as unprofessional and relatives may not discuss it out of fear of disbelief or even ridicule. What is important to remember is that someone's death is a totally unique experience, influenced by personal life experiences, religious beliefs, and/or spiritual beliefs as well as cultural backgrounds. Research has shown that these experiences are less uncommon than we might think and they happen in all religions and cultures, usually in the days or weeks before death. It is therefore crucial to adapt to the individual needs of the dying and to avoid the trap of imposing our own beliefs and assumptions about life and death. Above all, no one really knows what happens after death and there will always be a certain degree of mystery. Perhaps that is a good thing. To remain in a state of not-knowing, to stay open to the unexpected, the new, allows us to be open to potential insights and to have an increased awareness on or by the deathbed. Yet we do know that when the process of dying begins, we can discern a certain use of language and behaviour that deviates from what is considered normal. Learning to recognise, and become familiar with it can not only help the person dying, but also support the caregiver in making the transition easier.

> Whether dying persons are telling us of the glimpse of the next world or conversing with people we can't see, we should consider ourselves immensely blessed when it happens.
>
> If we don't make the mistake of assuming they are 'confused' we are likely to feel some of the excitement they convey.
>
> For we are witnessing the momentary merging of two worlds that at all other times remain tightly compartmentalised and mutually inaccessible.
>
> That merging is what I mean by the spirituality of death.[1]

---

[1] From: *Are They Hallucinations or Are They Real?*, Stafford L. Betty. Omega, 2006.

END-OF-LIFE
EXPERIENCES

In his research Fenwick talks about 'end-of-life experiences', the so-called ELEs[2]. In the following chapters I will also refer to ELEs, end-of-life experiences, where I previously used expressions such as deathbed phenomena, experiences, sightings, apparitions and phenomena together. Fenwick distinguishes between two categories of ELEs, the transpersonal ELE and the final meaning ELE.

Transpersonal end-of-life experiences

Transpersonal end-of-life experiences (ELEs) have a subtle, other-worldly quality. These ELEs seem not only to herald the approach of death but to also calm and alleviate the manner of dying. They cannot be simply and solely linked to the pathological process of dying, the physical process. Given that ELEs are culture-linked, people sometimes report that they have been visited by a religious figure associated with their own beliefs. A Christian might meet Jesus or Mary, while a Hindu might see Vishnu.

---

[2] Fenwick's research concentrates on the experiences of those who have died after a short or long-term illness and does not involve those who have died suddenly.

Examples of transpersonal ELEs

- Visions of dead relatives or religious figures who have come to help the dying during their dying process.

- Being able to transit from one reality to another, often in an atmosphere of love and light.

- Coincidences, experienced by those who are close to the person who is dying, but are physically separated from them. These often take place from a great distance and occur at the actual moment of death. People will, for example, say that they have been visited by the deceased who has come to tell them that they are alright.

- Other unusual or transcendent phenomena which happen at the moment of death, such as a change of temperature in the room, clocks that stop, and a subtle perception of dampness, vapour, mist, or images around the body. They are often accompanied by feelings of love, light, and comfort. Sometimes cats, dogs and birds will exhibit unusual behaviour.

- A presence in the room at some point after death, experienced by some nursing staff or carers, often described as a warm, loving atmosphere. Sometimes the atmosphere can be unpleasant and disturbing.

Whichever experience we are talking about, it is undeniable that it leaves a profound and unforgettable impression on those involved.

Final meaning end-of-life experiences

Final meaning end-of-life experiences are those which have a deep significance in the sense that they seem to encourage those who are about to die to deal with any unfinished business before the end. Resolving unfinished matters tends to ease existential worry and anxiety and allows the dying person to prepare spiritually for the approaching death.

Examples of final meaning ELEs

- A sudden desire to reconcile with relatives with whom they have lost touch, or to resolve personal or family matters.

- Unexpected lucid moments in people who until shortly before that moment are confused, semi-conscious or even completely unconscious. So clearheaded they are able to say goodbye to those around them.

- People who are unconscious or dying have the power to wait for the arrival or the departure of their loved ones before passing away.

- Profound dreams during sleep or waking moments that can help those involved come to terms with what has happened in their lives.

SPIRITUAL QUALITY OR HALLUCINATION?

Both transpersonal and final meaning ELEs seem to have a spiritual quality, such as feelings of hope, connection, and trust. The dying and those who witness these end-of-life experiences describe them in terms of compassion and reassurance, including loving, comforting, beautiful and preparatory. Sometimes the experiences can be frightening. However, in most cases ELEs are seen as being able to alleviate spiritual suffering and deep sorrow that will ease the transition into death. The feelings here seem to be in complete contrast to the fear and anxiety caused by hallucinations induced by medication, confusion or dementia.

Volunteer, Gon, talked about her experience with her dying father, which seemed to bring him no comfort at all, and her perception of what happened:

My father had non-Hodgkin lymphoma and refused to have any treatment. When he first heard the diagnosis, he was given 6 months to live. During his last month when he became increasingly weaker, he would lie on a chaise longue. I had noticed several times that he would suddenly sit up and stare intently towards the right-hand corner of the room. His eyes would nearly pop out of his head and seemed to say: What on earth am I seeing? I don't know for sure, but I thought that he was thinking: this just can't be ... because he would shake his head and close his eyes again to shut it out. Then he would just lie there with his eyes closed, not daring to open them again for a while, but then it seemed to happen again. He sat up slowly, it was as though he was in another world, shook his head again, closed his eyes then lay down again. This happened three times. He was so wrapped up in another world that I didn't dare to ask him anything, then or later. He was a very rational man, and I think he was experiencing something that he simply couldn't accept because it didn't make sense. He just couldn't believe it. It was so surprising for me, but I couldn't ask him about it because he was so withdrawn. Angry and withdrawn. But I was also thinking: This is holy, this is a special moment. I felt that he was in another world and really didn't know where he was. He also seemed to be experiencing a truly incredible moment, until his logical brain told him: this is impossible. Yes, for me it was a sacred moment, and intriguing because I couldn't see anything in the corner. I would have loved to know what he saw. I always hoped that it was his father, they had been very close.

His scepticism won. Well, of course I don't know for sure but that was my impression. I really didn't feel that it gave him any comfort. Perhaps it did comfort him, but he was resisting it with all his might. On the last day he couldn't get up at all but he kept on looking towards that corner. This time he didn't look surprised, he just looked at it.

How do we know that ELEs are not hallucinations? When you are familiar with ELEs, the difference between a genuine ELE and a drug-induced hallucination is fairly obvious. People who experience drug-induced hallucinations describe them as irritating hindrances, not specifically frightening but definitely annoying. These hallucinations can involve seeing animals walking around, children running in and out, devils or dragons dancing in the lights, insects crawling up the walls, or vague figures which seem to be moving in the carpet. Carers report that their patients grasp at the air and shiver. These kinds of hallucinations can disappear if the medication is changed. In contrast, transpersonal and final meaning end-of-life experiences occur mostly when the patient is fully aware and they seem to be powerful, personal experiences, that have huge significance for those experiencing them as well as for their relatives, friends, and carers. These end-of-life experiences seem to help the dying person to let go of the physical world,

and overcome their fear of death as well as often providing comfort for their nearest and dearest.

A palliative carer (GB):

> With drug-induced hallucinations] you see people going down to pick up things they can see crawling and that can happen over a couple of years. But...when you get a sense of this real inner peace, it feels more spiritual than hallucinations do. It's a different thing altogether.

Nurse Mieke:

> Deathbed phenomena are profound experiences, which involve contact with another dimension. Hallucinations are reactions to medication, or for example, a shortage of oxygen, dehydration and the like.

Volunteer Anke sometimes has difficulty distinguishing between drug-induced hallucinations and these specific end-of-life experiences:

> You see, people who hallucinate often see spiders, which you then have to catch. To me, these are typical cases of hallucination. When it concerns loved ones who have already died it's clear to me as well, but when it's about unidentifiable figures, then it's harder to tell. I still take it seriously, of course I do, because who am I to say that it isn't true. In the latter case, I perceive people as more confused than those who clearly told me that they saw someone they knew beside the bed. But not so confused that I think: this is a hallucination.

It is important to bear in mind that someone who is dying, who looks confused or acts incoherently, can be in the process of coming to terms with a powerful, subjective experience inside that confusion, which is called terminal anxiety.

The impact of dementia on the process of dying can be even more confusing and possibly alarming. Dementia and seriously damaged cognitive functions are an increasing problem amongst our aging population. According to the Alzheimer Foundation in the Netherlands, at least one in five Dutch people suffers from some form of dementia. In these cases it can be difficult and sometimes even impossible to connect with the dying person or understand what he or she is saying or wants. To maintain contact, it helps us if we realise that he or she is going through an inner and very personal process and we don't have to understand everything that is happening. However, studies have shown that those with severe dementia can suddenly become lucid enough to say farewell to loved ones or talk coherently about seeing deceased relatives. It requires a high degree of sensitivity on the part of carers and relatives not to dismiss them as incoherent ramblings. How wonderful it would be if we could be attentive and available if and when the dying person has a moment of clarity and wants to connect with us one last time.

Annelies talking about her deceased mother:

> What touched me very deeply was the process my mother went through. My mother was 87 and had been suffering from dementia for several years, then had a brain aneurism and was admitted to a nursing home. She was someone who took life as it came, whatever happened. She was very serene in the nursing home. She was turned from side to side, but she was so at peace that I thought: oh, how can you put up with this? Her life was over. She said this to me and my sister more than once. On the last day, she told her carer: 'I'm going to see Freek.' Freek was my father. Then: 'He is longing for me. I am going to cross over.' That's what Mum said. Plain and simple. My mother was a bit spiritual. Then she said: 'Phone the children.' They called me and my sister, and that's when my mother died. She didn't have any fever or pneumonia, she wasn't ill at all.

HOSPICE CAREGIVERS' EXPERIENCES

In the following chapters about the different kinds of end-of-life experiences, we will focus on the stories of the hospice caregivers themselves. Although it is the hospice caregivers who are talking about the phenomena experienced by the dying, and the experiences they themselves might have had, it's important to realise that the dying person is central here and that this is about their observations and experiences. The question of whether or not a hospice worker is able to see light, hear inner voices, smell specific odours, or sense energies, is not really important. It might indicate special sensitivities, but says nothing about the intuitive treatment know-how that hospice caregivers may or may not be capable of. Doing the right things when it matters rather than just doing it right. It is also worth stressing that these specific ELEs happen to about ten percent of people dying. For those going through it, dying is first and foremost a physical process. Also, most of the hospice residents suffer from some form of cancer. They have been through many exhausting chemotherapies and other treatments which often have disturbing side effects and devastating results. It is an intensely physical process that can possess the person dying completely and can be a real struggle. It is a process that can also evoke an instinctive fear, because in spite of all the treatment options, in a situation like this we have far less say than we would like to believe about what is happening to our bodies. So, as well as the pleasant experiences, dying also has its distressing, frightening, and less agreeable sides. In order to be better prepared I have included a chapter called 'Dealing with death,' which discusses these aspects.

Until now we have talked about nursing staff, caregivers, and attendants in general. This chapter concentrates specifically on those who took part in Fenwick's study carried out in the Netherlands between 2009 and 2011. Among the participants are a substantial number of volunteers. Volunteers who work in a hospice have a great deal of life experience. They are highly skilled in communication, devoted and yet detached when they need to be. Not everyone is suited to be a volunteer in a hospice. It calls for a special mentality, for dedication and understanding. Consciously or unconsciously, hospice caregivers have their own specific incentives to be involved in care for the dying. Sometimes it turns out that they have something they need to finish off in their own lives. This is how a Jewish volunteer came to terms with what had happened in her own life by caring for a Jewish resident. None of her family survived the war and for years she had felt guilty about being the only survivor. Caring for a resident led to understanding and mitigation for another volunteer. It enabled her to become reconciled with her own mother, now deceased, with whom she had had a disturbed relationship since she was a child. Sometimes being a volunteer is a direct result of a death in the family.

Floortje talks about her work as a volunteer:

> I think it has something to do with the death of my husband several years before. I think I was afraid of being near the dead. I found my husband when he died totally unexpectedly. In the days leading up to the funeral, he lay in our bedroom at home. I was with him a lot and slept in the same room. On the day of the funeral, I was in the garden with a deep sense of grief. The garden had always been very important to us. Then suddenly I felt that he was there with me. He was just there. I thought; how is this possible? I went straight into the bedroom. He had been there the whole time, but I just felt that he wasn't really there, that his body was an empty shell. Later I was so pleased that I had this experience because otherwise I couldn't have said my last goodbyes with peace of mind. Death will always be a mystery, but this...this was a harrowing experience. This is why I decided to come and work here. I would also like to know what it's like to actually be near the dead.

There are also people who want to grow, to develop themselves, who want to take a step towards inner growth. This is why new volunteers are always asked: What is it you bring with you? And just as important, what it is it you are coming to get? Being conscious of this is an absolute must in the care of the dying. Hospice volunteers also receive special training in their duties.

Aside from the volunteers, which was the largest group of participants in the study, nurses, supervisors, complementary care nurses[3] and a music therapist also took part.

Whereas the dying in hospitals or institutions are regarded as patients, in hospices they are called residents. Some hospices refer to them as guests. The latter is more commonly used in the so-called high care-hospices[4] than in those we would see as home-from-home-hospices.[5] There is an essential difference in the description, and therefore implicitly in the treatment, if we see the dying as a resident rather than a guest. If we ask ourselves who is actually the guest, we could perhaps conclude that it's the hospice caregivers who are the guests of the dying.

Thus, the dying are residents. This makes a difference to how hospice caregivers approach their work. You provide a service for a guest, for a resident, you are at their service. Being a service provider is a one-way street. A service provider is aiming for a specific result. Giving guidance for the dying is serving for the sake of the service itself. For the sake of love. Service is then a reciprocal process and is always founded on wholeness. In this book, the dying are residents of the three participating hospices. On occasion, hospice caregivers talk candidly about personal experiences with their own families or friends.

When we are in hospital as patients, most of us are focussing on

---

[3] Complementary care, sometimes called alternative care, is non-medical and/or nursing care for the dying. This can include massage, painting, harp music, use of essential oils or aromatherapy. Complementary care can enhance treatment for those who want it. It provides support and helps them in their journey towards death. Complementary care has therefore acquired a significant place and meaning in the care of the dying.

[4] Unlike the home-from-home hospices, the high care-hospices employ a variety of professional staff. This can vary from a doctor to a psychologist or a spiritual counsellor, from a physiotherapist or nurse to a volunteer.

[5] home-from-home hospices try to recreate the home situation as much as possible and do not have medical or nursing staff in attendance. The staff are mainly volunteers. The medical responsibility remains with the GP and nursing care is provided by homecare.

our recovery and thus on our treatment. The treatment is often unnecessarily protracted, encouraged by the medical staff who perhaps see death as a failure, but just as much by the insistence of the patients themselves and/or by family and friends. There seem to be four major justifications for ongoing or overtreatment according to an online poll, which the *Medisch Contact* (a medical journal for doctors) sent to 1,600 panel members of The Royal Dutch Medical Association (KNMG).[6] Doctors are treatment-orientated and want to treat their patients as they have been trained to do (said 53%). The patient's expectations of the treatment are too high (51%) and he doesn't take it into account that he might die (45%). Finally, the families want the doctor to do everything in his or her power to keep their loved ones alive (46%). Without passing judgement on the matter, we could perhaps suggest that as long as we stay focussed on treatment, the inner preparation for death remains unattended, while in that precious and essential process of dying, inner preparation has its own special place and significance. The patient is deprived of exactly that at the moment when overtreatment is chosen.

When it becomes clear that there is no point in further treatment, we say that the patient is getting worse. Even in hospices, when death is within sight, some tend to say that someone is getting worse or that the person is deteriorating. However hospices are in fact places where people die. Very rarely do patients get well and actually leave a hospice. This is confusing for those involved and most certainly not easy to deal with, especially for the dying when they are admitted to a hospice. Because, surely, that is why they are there. So, that being the case, I would advocate that there be no more mention of getting worse or deteriorating, but rather that someone's physical strength is waning or that the dying are approaching the end of life. My experiences as a volunteer and hospice supervisor have taught me that dying transcends our understanding of and opinions about "worse" and "better". Not getting better physically does not mean that one cannot be healed.

---

[6] *Medisch Contact* | 1st. June 2012 | 67 nr. 22 1326-13-29. You will find the full results of this poll and more information about this subject on www.medischcontact.nl. The Royal Dutch Medical Association (KNMG) is the Netherlands' medical Federation.

VISIONS AND
DREAMS

Visions and dreams are perhaps the most frequently reported ELEs. This was also the case in the study carried out in the Netherlands. In most visions, the dying see deceased loved ones with whom they had a close relationship. Their purpose seems to be to help the dying through the process. These encounters also seem to spiritually prepare the dying for death. In these cases, the dying talk about someone coming to collect them, going with someone, going away or going on a journey.

Volunteer, Diny, talks about her experience with her mother:

My mother suddenly turned to my daughter and said 'Would you go and pack my bag, because Jan is waiting for me.' Jan was her husband and she could see him. She also saw other members of the family, but not her mother. It was really about her husband because he died at a relatively young age, he was only 52. My mother was 85. She could see her husband and she knew that she was going to be with him. We thought that it was so beautiful. My daughter did indeed pretend to pack her bag. She died about a day and a half later.

I had a similar experience with my husband. We asked him: 'Oh, can you see any of the family? Can you see your youngest sister?' 'No,' he replied, 'I can't see her but I can see my mother and my father, and my two aunts who brought me up.' We were able to ask these direct questions because in Italy, where my husband was from, they have a different attitude than the people here. For instance, they always leave a window open so the soul can leave. The front door will be open so everyone can walk in. In Italy, it's accepted that when you die, you will see loved ones who have already passed on. I think it gave my husband comfort; yes, I'm sure it did. For us, it was a sign that it would happen very soon and that he would see his family again when he died.

Volunteer Anke talks about a lady who was in the process of dying, but who was not ready to go. She thought that she might be taken before she was ready. She was in denial and kept saying:

'I'm not ready yet' and 'I don't want to go yet'. She told us that an uncle of hers was nearby. This uncle had died some time ago and was a gravedigger when he was alive. He was constantly on her mind. She would talk about him and kept saying: 'He's here you know, he's really here. He's here with me and I think I have to go with him.' She thought it was a clear sign that he was with her. And that he would be taking her any time soon.

Eventually I had a sense that she was at peace, and that she was fine with the idea that he was nearby. It brought a degree of acceptance. In the middle of all the protests, there was acceptance. She was able to describe it really well. We talked about it a lot, even though she was quite reserved, and came to enjoy our chats very much. We were both very puzzled about this fellow hanging around.

These visions and dreams are often seen as reassuring and comforting experiences.

Volunteer, Gineke, says:

Dreams happen a lot. People have wonderful dreams in which they are already 'up there' and say how beautiful it is. It's also an easy and nice question: 'how did you sleep?' And: 'did you dream?' That gives them an opening to talk about what happened. Actually, residents often say that they've seen people who have died and that they have met them. What it was like? Wonderful. It makes people happy and they want to talk about it.

Gineke goes on to talk about a resident who often dreamed about her husband who had died and that she really wanted to go with him:

I often worked the early shift from 7 till 11. One day I went in to see Lenie. I could see that she was rather sad and asked her: 'What's the matter, did you have a bad night?' She answered: 'My husband, my husband who died, he sat on my bed and came to pick me up but I'm still here.' She had so wanted to go with him. In fact, she had a long way to go before she, at last, could go with him. She actually left the hospice. That was one of my first experiences in this hospice of people telling me about seeing their loved ones and families who had come to collect them.

Nurse Willy shares her thoughts:

For me, visions are, for instance, when people say they can see a light in the corner of the room or that they have dreamed about their husband who has died and who sits on the edge of their bed. There are also people who say: 'Could you just shut that window, it's a bit draughty', when the window is actually closed. I clearly remember a lady who's mind was totally clear, awake and not confused. She told me: 'I know I'll be going to a good place when I die. I have faith in it and I know it's true. There are my friends, my family and others who are waving and clapping because I'm on my way to them.' When she died, we found a lovely poem which was about a boat sailing off into the distance, and reappearing in another place. For me, this was a very enlightening experience.

Volunteer, Lisette, also talks about a similar experience:

One of our residents told us that she had been somewhere else, where there were lots of people, that it was very busy. The way she described it, it sounded like it was a busy marketplace or square with pavement cafes: 'there are people everywhere and I am walking among them, and I can see lots of people I know.' I didn't say anything, I just let her talk. I didn't ask: 'Are your father and mother there?' For me it was a beautiful and very special experience.

Nurse Cocky:

I clearly remember a lady and her son, a man in his fifties. He worked in business and was rational in his thinking. He was sitting by his mother's deathbed when she suddenly said: 'There's Henk.' It turned out that Henk was her husband and the man's father. This was a totally new and therefore very special experience for her son, as it was for me too because I was there. When you see how someone suddenly says something like that, you haven't the nerve to cast doubts. That's just how it is. She said it in such a matter-of–fact way that even that highly logical man didn't doubt her. It was just so straightforward. I've had more of these experiences. There was the lady who saw a whole row of people, all sitting on her bed. She was able to describe it so clearly. It gave her comfort, actually brought her peace of mind. The reassurance: that's where I'm going.

Nurse Wilma talks about Liesbeth, a young woman with mental disabilities

I want to tell you about Liesbeth, one of our residents who had come from an institution for the intellectually challenged, although she could read and write. A young woman with metastasized cancer who also had epileptic seizures. She deteriorated very quickly. She was angry and truly lived from within her emotions. Everything was either black or white. But she could also be very affectionate and warm. One day she was terribly upset because she had lost her handkerchief, a red handkerchief. She told me 'It's my father's and he's very cross.' 'But your father is dead, isn't he?' I asked. 'Yes,' she replied, 'but he comes to visit me every evening.' So we started to talk about her father. He came every evening to see how she was, talked to her and told her a bedtime story. She wasn't confused at all, quite clear in her mind as a matter of fact and also told others about her experiences; to my colleagues and her family. Her father was simply there. She died shortly after this. Peacefully. She was an asset to the hospice, a beautiful experience.

These visions not only seem to prepare the dying for approaching death, they can also be healing experiences. Volunteer Anke talks about a woman whose child had died at the age of eighteen, and had now come back to be with her mother:

This lady found great comfort in the fact that her daughter knew she was coming. She believed that she would be collected, so dying no longer worried her. It was a very encouraging and comforting experience. It also gave her a chance to talk about her child. It was clear that she was in touch with her. I let her talk about who her daughter was

34

and what it was like at the time, when she died. She told me so much, while all the time her daughter was present with us during our talks.

The feeling that her daughter was coming to collect her was encouraging and comforting for this mother while in her process of dying. It was also a wonderful opportunity to talk about her daughter.

Anke went on:

> I remember that this lady had been unable to talk to her husband about the death of her daughter. She told me: 'I can't speak about her with my husband, he dealt with her death in a completely different way and he would think this was crazy.' She didn't dare to share it with him because she was afraid of being judged.

Supervisor Simone tells me about Rita, who died supported by palliative sedation:

> In the weeks she stayed with us and lay here waiting – because that's how she saw it – she told us a great deal. She had lost her father when she was fourteen and her mother simply couldn't cope. Rita took on a lot of responsibility and had to deal with so much, and that's how she had felt all her life: I must be strong. She found all the kindness and shelter she received here very challenging and hard to accept.

> She had always felt her father was near her, but when she was in the hospice, she couldn't feel him anymore. She noted his absence soberly and hoped he would be with her at the moment she died. Eventually, she was sedated and just before the sedation took effect she said: 'I can feel him again now.' It was a comforting experience but she didn't get overexcited, for her it was a reality, nothing out of the ordinary.

As we mentioned before, ELEs also seem to contain a cultural element. People who have a solid religious background sometimes meet relious figures from their own traditional beliefs. For Christians this could be Jesus or Mary, and also angels may appear. You also come across this phenomenon during supervised meditations, where people are asked to make a connection with someone who holds a spiritual meaning for them. It's striking that, even when people haven't practised their faith for many years, they will find a figure from their original belief system appearing in their thoughts.

Winifred, volunteer:

One of our residents kept trying to grab something out of the air, but it didn't seem to be the hoist handle above her bed. She kept moving her hand in the air and from time to time her whole face was transformed. I can't really describe it, but her face seemed to light up and then she called out: 'Mary, Mary.'

Volunteer Cok tells about a gentleman from an orthodox background:

I came into his room and asked if he wanted me to close the curtains. He told me there were three angels by the window, but I was welcome to close the curtains. The angels would disappear but they would come back. He was used to it. Many years before, he had had an accident. There were angels there too but they told him he had to go back for a while. It was so surprising that this gentleman could say this as though it was nothing unusual. You wouldn't have expected him to, given his background. For him it was quite normal and familiar and was really part of his reality. He was definitely not confused.

Volunteer Suzanne talks about an experience she had never been able to talk about before:

I was sitting at the bedside of a resident when the figure of Jesus Christ appeared on the wall. My fellow volunteer José saw it too, but we never said a word. The gentleman died, the supervisor and the family arrived, and I went home. The next day I was on duty again and I heard other volunteers say: 'That's odd, it's as if one of the apostles is lying here.' And: 'Oh yes, he really could have been one of Jesus' disciples.' I heard this in the hospice being said by people to whom I had never told what I had seen. Later I talked to José about it and she said: 'Yes, yes, it really was him, it was Jesus.' But I was still rather embarrassed because of my resistance towards the Christian religion, but it was true. And imagine, the fact that others actually see the deceased as an apostle! I now have the courage to talk about it.

Nurse Mieke remembers:

There was a situation with one of our residents, which I still remember so well to this day. He rang for me and I went to see him. He was lying

36

in bed, beaming and happy. He said to me: 'I've just seen God, and now I know that I can die in peace.' This gentleman was so peaceful, there was such a feeling of tranquillity all around him, he was just so happy. I wanted to ask him so much more about it, but I didn't. I really regret that now. I accepted it. Yes, it was still so clearly around him that I could almost see it. I think I was just so overwhelmed because I found it so beautiful. All I could do was experience it. It obviously brought him peace. As I think about it, I can still feel it. It was an experience that left a huge impression on me.

Volunteer Helen talks about her father, a religious man:

He was prepared for his transition by a revelation rather than a vision. My father had a rock-solid belief and faith. He knew where he was going. He was also longing to go Home. My father had found my mother's death very hard. She suffered a brain haemorrhage and was gone in an instant. One day she was celebrating her birthday, the next day she died. At one point my father called me and said: 'Your Mum is in heaven, it was revealed to me by the Lord.' A verse from one of the psalms suddenly came to him and he knew: Mum was in Heaven. He truly believed that. That's when we, his children, could also say: 'Then everything is alright.' I think that he really longed to be with her, but for him the Lord was most important. I do believe that you will be reunited with loved ones in Heaven, but my father didn't discuss this with me. I was convinced that my father had an intuition which gave him this knowledge, this inner certainty. The Lord had revealed it to him.

It is well known that the dying are sometimes taken to another reality by their loved ones. It's a reality which is usually perceived as more real than our normal reality. A reality imbued with light, love and compassion. This reality often leads to an expansion of the spiritual vision of the dying, and holds a promise that there is life after death.

Volunteer Cok:

The very first evening I came to work in the hospice, there was a lady who was dying and the nurse asked if I would sit with her, which I did. I sat there quietly and could hear life going on as usual outside the room, while the lady was deeply asleep. After a while, about an hour and a half later, the nurse came in. We stood there talking softly. Suddenly the lady looked up, ever so radiantly, to her left, then her right, then left and right again and then her smile left her face and she said, rather disappointedly: 'Oh, I thought I was already in heaven.' For a short moment she was with us again. I believe she died the next morning. For me it was strange. I thought: does this happen every time you come here? Yes, it was a nice start.

Sometimes visions can definitively help people to come to terms with the life they have lived. Carer Wilma tells us about two such remarkable examples: one involving a resident with ALS[7] and a war trauma, and another resident who was never allowed to accept her sexual orientation during her lifetime. It's impressive when we realise how much is still possible in the last stages of our lives, and how healing it can be for those involved.

Nurse Wilma:

> She was the first ALS patient who we had looked after here. We weren't sure how much care she needed. I was with her a great deal in the final days. She could only point and had a voice computer. She was half-Jewish, half-German. This caused a lot of tension between her parents during Hitler's rise to power, which affected her whole life. She suffered an incredible war trauma. Yet during her final days, she had a perception which allowed her to make peace with her parents. I don't know whether or not she actually saw her parents but she changed. I said to her: 'Goodness you look so different, do you feel different?' She began to type, telling about her past and she 'told' me that she had understood from her parents that everything was alright now. So she was able to be reconciled with her past at the very end of her life. I could see that, because she looked so different. She was a woman who never looked straight at you, she would avoid your eyes. Now her eyes had changed and she could look me in the eye. More friendly. Liberated. The hurt was gone, all she had left was the physical pain. Her children noticed it too. But she found it hard to discuss it with her family, except with her daughter. She told me that she had read a Christmas story to her mother in German. It meant so much to her.

---

[7] ALS is a progressive neurodegenerative disease and stands for amyotrophic lateral sclerosis.

The daughter had the feeling that her mother changed while she was reading the story, that she could relive the good parts of her childhood.

We also had a lady staying with us who was seventy years old, and still talked about her mother. She had had a difficult life. She was lesbian but could never express it openly. And so she got married. She had always had problems with her mother. On her final day, when she was almost slipping away, she suddenly stretched out her arms and said: 'Mum, is everything alright? Have you come to get me? Is it alright if I come up there soon?' It wasn't a hallucination. Her children were there and it was also a healing experience for them, because they had lived with the tension between their mother and grandmother for many years.

COINCIDENCES AND
SYNCHRONICITY

I t's remarkable how often people suddenly have the sensation that someone with whom they have a close and meaningful connection, has died. It then turns out that this someone died at the very moment they had that sensation. Those involved often live far apart from each other, as in Christina's case (page 7). Such sensations often come in a dream, just between sleeping and waking or when someone wakes up suddenly. It's as though the loved one has come to say goodbye and to reassure the other that all is well with him or her.

Volunteer Cok:

> My mother was a very down-to-earth woman, she had always worked hard and had no time for anything out of the ordinary. Even so, she once told me that she had seen my older sister, her daughter, who had died. She said: 'It might sound odd, but I've seen Geertje' I asked her: 'Really?' She replied 'Yes, and it wasn't just a dream... I was just resting on the couch. It was like a white apparition and full of light. I couldn't see her face but it was really her and she just came to say hello. I already thought that she was alright but now I know for sure.' It did her so much good; just that confirmation for my mother that it was alright.

It is much less common for this to happen when people are in a state of fully waking consciousness. Although music therapist Hilly told me about what happened to her.

> I had an experience that was very significant in my life. It happened when I was still working as a doctor and was attending a conference in Florence. I was walking down the street and suddenly there was this apparition, hovering about half a metre above the ground. It was one of my husband's friends, whom I didn't know well but did get on rather well with. He told me that he was fine. It only lasted for a few moments. I knew he had cancer, but I thought he still had two or three months to live.
>
> That same evening I was in my hotel when my husband called. He told me that this friend had died. It happened that afternoon, so he had appeared to me several hours before his death. That day, I had just carried on as normal. Apparently my everyday mind couldn't seem to accept what had happened. It was only when I got the phone call that the image of his apparition came back to me. I told my husband about it straight away. He knew I had had these kinds of experiences before and could listen without judgement. It was very enriching for me.

Nurse Mieke with an example of a 'coincidence' and how taking part in this study made her even more aware:

> A couple of weeks ago one of our residents died, which happened quite quickly. In fact, it was quite sudden and I had to call the family. I called the grandson, who had the most contact with him. I said: 'Your grandfather has passed away. I'm sorry to have to let you know by telephone.' 'Oh,' he answered, 'that's fine, I already knew. I had such a pain in my eye.' 'What time was that?' 'ten to four', he replied, and I told him: 'That's the time your grandfather died.' Unlike the earlier experiences, I could talk about it because I was busy with the questionnaire for this study. I really should have asked him about the pain in his eye. But I found it so overwhelming you know; I just told him 'What a lovely experience!' Because he associated the feeling with his grandfather straight away, which is why he was so sure.

42

Supervisor Suzanne tells me about a lady who had been an emergency admission, and an experience with her grandson:

Her two very lovely daughters were with her when she arrived. They had gone through such turmoil and worry in the hospital. It was so good to see her and her children settle down in our hospice, and that they could still enjoy their time together. The special bond that this lady had with her grandson became apparent in the most remarkable way. Her grandson dreamt that he saw his grandmother. She came towards him, and he wanted to get up and say hello. She pushed him away, back into his pillow. He woke up crying and ran to his mother. That very moment we called her to say that his grandmother had died. It was half past one in the morning. Grandma had come to say goodbye to her grandson.

Sometimes very strange transcendental phenomena occur at or around the moment of death. When two or more of these events take place almost simultaneously, we call it synchronicity. Events that can't be seen as cause and effect in the strictest sense, but which are similar or related in meaning. One example is when clocks stop at the moment a person dies. The following is a truly remarkable event that happened around the time of death.

Nurse Cocky:

A long time ago, we had a really special lady who stayed with us for some time. She eventually passed away, but this also took a long time. We sat with her, a woman all alone, her husband had already passed on and they had no children. She had a sister who came to visit. We were sitting at the end of her bed. Just as she was about to die, her bedside table rose off the floor. I nudged M. and said: 'Look at that.' It sank back to the floor and it was as though nothing had happened. I saw it quite clearly. We never talked about it again. I didn't take the incident any further; I wouldn't have known what to do. I do know that she was a very unique lady and that this had something to do with what happened. With her being taken. The feeling in the room was one of serenity, calm. She was also peaceful, it wasn't a struggle. A very special experience.

Simone, supervisor:

We recently experienced this stopping of clocks with a gentleman. His wife noticed it afterwards. It happened one morning, fifteen minutes before he died. His watch stopped at a quarter to nine. Now, this was special because his wife had given him this watch thirty years ago. A very handsome watch with a worn strap. He never took it off, but now it was lying next to his bed.

At some point that morning she had said: 'I'm just going into the conservatory to watch the sun come up.' While she was there, he died. They had always talked a lot about the light. She was at peace too and didn't think: oh no, I missed it. It felt right because she watched the sun rise at the exact moment he died. Everything was so in tune.

Volunteer Lisette:

One of our residents had died at a particular time. Family members told us that at the moment of his death, late one evening, the crucifix he had given them fell of the wall. The whole family were there and they said: 'Oh look, Uncle Jan's just letting us know he's still here', but that was the very moment that he died.

Another gentleman died while his son was visiting him. His wife had stayed at home with the children because she couldn't find a babysitter. The son called to tell her: 'He has died.' 'What time was that?' she asked from their home. 'Half past eleven.' 'My goodness, how strange, our clock stopped at half past eleven '

Supervisor Suzanne about a lady who clearly felt that her death was approaching:

We had a lady in the hospice whose brother came to visit every day. This lady didn't want to die yet. She had brought her coat to the hospice, because she thought she would still be able to get out a bit. One day she said: 'You can take my coat back home.' Her brother was really surprised. Then she said: 'You can take my cardigan as well.' Her brother was even more surprised because it was her favourite cardigan. At that moment it didn't seem as if this lady was going to die, but that evening she was gone. When I called the brother to tell him the news, he told me that he already knew: on the way home he had been listening to the car radio and he heard a German religious song, 'Alles ist vergangen', meaning everything is gone.

Volunteer, Annelies:

I remember a resident who had been with us for quite some time, an unmarried man. We got on so well, Bas and I. We had the same rather dark sense of humour. I was always popping in to see him and he would always ask: 'When are you coming back?' He had lost so much weight. He had lived a full life right up to the end but now he was exhausted. I was allowed to keep watch with his brother and sister-in-law. We were sitting round him when the two burning candles that were standing on a small table in between us suddenly went out, one after the other. While we were looking at these candles we heard a sigh. Bas had died. All three of us just sat there, unable to move: This is a miracle, it's a sign. No, it's impossible ... The doors were closed, there was no draught in the room. For me it was a beautiful sign ...

When we talk about coincidences and synchronicity, it seems that people often see birds and butterflies. While I was combining my work as a hospice volunteer with my practice for the dying, bereavement and grief counselling, I was sitting with a dying woman and observed the following. She was singing softly to herself. Sometimes she would look at me without really seeing me. She seemed to be calling something softly to her: 'Red', ... 'green', she sang, then again 'red', 'green'. She seemed to be getting impatient, but there was still that quiet, long-drawn-out call: 'Re-e-d, gree-n ...' She really was in another world because when I asked what she was looking at, she didn't answer. The lady died the next day. Both daughters asked me to give the eulogy at their mother's funeral. I was very honoured to carry out this task in my other capacity. On the day of the funeral, I was walking through the beautiful, tree-filled cemetery on my way to the chapel when all of a sudden I saw a woodpecker ... the sight of that green bird with its red head has since often filled my head with wonder.

Volunteer Tina tells her story:

I would regularly visit a lady who had spent some time here in the hospice but who later left us. I visited her until she died. When I went

45

in to say goodbye for the last time, I told her: 'Anne, you'll come back as a little bird in my garden.' It spontaneously came out. It was such a lovely image in my mind ... yes, I just said it. A few weeks after she died I experienced something. It was in the morning and I was lying in bed, reading. Now this was remarkable in itself, because it was through books that I had become so close to Anne. I had brought her various books and we would always talk about them. She knew that I always read in bed between 8 and 9 o'clock every morning. That morning at half past eight, a little bird flew into my bedroom. My bedroom is divided in two parts and in one there is a sash window that was open a few inches. The bird swooped into the other part of the bedroom and flew straight out through the small upper window on the other side. I sat there in bed, stunned. Anne popped up in my mind straight away. If you knew my bedroom you wouldn't believe that the little bird could find its way out. That was the strangest part. I mean, sure, I see birds in my garden all the time. I often see a robin in my garden and think: could that be Anne? That's different. But this ... at first I panicked a bit. I thought: that bird will never find its way out, what should I do? This experience left a huge impression on me. It was simply a beautiful experience for me. Especially because I had told her: 'You'll come back as a bird.' It was that combination. Me saying it was already strange enough.

The idea that someone could see their deceased loved one or someone they were close to as a bird is not so strange. It is primarily the sensory experience combined with the sighting that makes it so meaningful for those involved. You will find more about birds acting as messengers for impending death further on in this book in the chapter 'Dogs, cats and birds'. Just like birds, butterflies also appeal to the imagination when it comes to coincidences and synchronicity.

Volunteer Diny tells the following story:

After my husband died we kept on seeing a butterfly. It had brown wings with orange spots. I was standing in the kitchen talking to my daughter when it flew in, and it kept coming back. Sometime later we went to Italy to visit my husband's family, and there it was again. My sister-in-law said: 'this isn't the right time for butterflies.' But I saw it there twice. I definitely associate it with my husband. Without any doubt. It was at the cemetery too for a while.

The butterfly is symbolic in many cultures.[8] On the one hand it can be a symbol of transformation and beauty, and on the other of the transience of joy and the brevity of life. The butterfly evokes joy and lightness in us and is the symbol of the process of transformation and metamorphosis. The changing appearance of the butterfly in its three stages is a true miracle and captures many peoples' imagination. It gives us the hope that transformation is possible. Hope that we can be transformed from our earthly existence to a world of light and immortality. The soul emerges from its bodily shell, just like a butterfly from its cocoon. Christians believe the soul will go through three stages: life, death and resurrection. It is therefore no surprise that the butterfly is seen as a symbol of death on many gravestones, past and present. In her book Tijd van sterven (*Time of dying*)[9] Almut Bockemühl describes this process of metamorphosis beautifully:

> I was wandering through the tall grass when I saw a white butterfly flitting about. He was dancing in the wind in front of my eyes and then disappeared behind some bushes. We have devised so many images to describe the process of dying. One of the most beautiful is that of the butterfly, which sheds its cocoon, the superfluous earthly shell and flies up towards the sun like a delicate creature of light. Just as you wouldn't want to force a butterfly back into its cocoon, you wouldn't want to call back an old or sick person who has crossed the threshold. Everything becomes new at the moment of death. A human being is just like the butterfly when he dies. But in his bondage to the earth in the earlier stages of life, does he not already remind us of a caterpillar, creeping along the ground endlessly collecting food and stuffing himself? Let us not look down on the caterpillar with disdain, for he is the child of the butterfly. The butterfly goes through a number of stages and the caterpillar is one of them. Remember that it doesn't suddenly change from one form to another. There are enigmatic transitional forms that move in between, where an entire life is set within; the egg and the cocoon. These forms are helpless and motionless, yet inside the most

---

[8] Hans Biedermann (1991). *Symbolen. Historisch-culturele symbolen van A tot Z (Symbols. Historical-cultural symbols from A to Z)* Utrecht: Het Spectrum. *Dictionary of Symbolism: Cultural Icons & the Meaning Behind Them.*

[9] Almut Bockemühl (1993). *Tijd van sterven (Time of dying). A daughter describes the last stages of her mother's death.* Zeist: Vrij Geestesleven. (Not published in English)

profound changes are taking place. Don't these stages have parallels in the life of man, for example the first few months of life and extreme old age? But it's in these transitional periods that extraordinary things are experienced and accomplished, in a situation where help and care is urgently needed.

There are several transitional periods in our lives: puberty, leaving home, becoming a parent, retirement, just to name a few. Christine Longaker[10] tells us that the characteristic of a transition is that it creates an opening in our seemingly unmovable reality. An opening which gives us the opportunity to change, to revise our attitudes, to take a new direction, to detach ourselves from the material world, to tune into and come closer to our innermost selves. We can also see death as a kind of transition. When we see death as a transition, then we might learn to consider that dying, by its very nature, might 'accomplish extraordinary things' or might bring about 'the most profound changes'. Realising this could be one of the most important aspects in the care of the dying. Then the question arises, is it up to us to intervene, or should we simply respect the process as it happens and provide the best support we can. Just to be there and to stay close.

Esther, a client at my practice, told me about her vision of a 'butterfly-like figure'. A vision that prepared her for the death of her twin sister:

The night before I was due to fly back to the Netherlands from Greece to be with my twin sister, who had suddenly fallen very ill, I had a vision. We had stayed up late dining with friends, and had to get up early in the morning to drive to the airport in Athens. I hadn't been asleep for long when I suddenly woke up at two in the morning. I saw Yvette lying very still and then, rising up out of her body, a butterfly-like figure appeared and flew away. I was convinced that Yvette had died. When I called the next morning from the airport, one of my sisters assured me that if Yvette had died during the night, the hospital would have phoned. I saw Yvette that afternoon. Her face was pale; her lips were white, but she was still alive. I told her about my vision.

---

[10] Christine Longaker (1997). *Het licht van afscheid. Hoop vinden in leven en sterven. Een leidraad voor emotionele en spirituele zorg.* Amsterdam: De Boekerij. *(Facing Death and Finding Hope; A Guide to the Emotional and Spiritual Care of the Dying.)*

'Indeed, I'm already dead', she replied. 'Why are you still here then?', I asked, rather cheekily. 'Saying goodbye', she answered. 'Not to you, I've already done that. No, I'm giving you the chance to say goodbye to me.' And that's what happened. Over the next two days, our parents, sisters and her friends all sat round her bed and she was perfectly approachable. Then she died.

'After death, a person is like a butterfly', says Bockemühl. Held in this light, Yvette's reaction had significant meaning when Esther said she believed her sister was already dead because she had seen the butterfly-like figure rising out of Yvette's body and flying away. Yvette had replied 'Indeed, I'm already dead', indicating that she actually looked like that butterfly. She only stayed because she wanted to give her family the chance to say goodbye to her.

THE TRANSITION
TO NEW REALITIES

As part of the process, the dying seem to be able to transit from one reality to another. Sometimes they themselves say that they were somewhere else, but family and hospice caregivers notice it too.

Nurse Willy talks about this moving back and forth between different realities and how she manages it:

Some people look away, for example, they don't make eye contact anymore and fix their gaze towards somewhere halfway up the wall; they might hear your voice but they don't really see you. Then they come out of it again. They say: 'Oh, everything was just so peaceful, I was so calm ... it was so lovely, but now I'm back.' I can really tell when people are somewhere else for a while. Sometimes the family want to call them back, but then I might say: 'She's so peaceful, just try sitting there quietly and see what happens.' On occasion, if I see that someone is looking away from us, I might say that they are walking along a different path, and that although we want him here with us, he seems to know where he's going. If the family isn't used to seeing this, it's up to me to try to reassure them about what is happening, to help them understand that it's all part of the process. It can also be difficult for the family if their loved one is restless and they immediately want you to change the medication. If I can reassure them by saying that it's all part of letting go, that the struggle is part of it, then I notice that the family find it easier to accept what's happening. It's a comforting thought when there's someone there who is familiar with this process, who can tell them what's happening. I can tell them that it's a necessary part in the process of dying. That's really important, because otherwise they'll just ask for more medication. Of course we try to still their fears but it really is quite natural.

Volunteer Anke's story about a resident who described the relationship between the body and the spirit so clearly and how the two were connected:

She told me that she felt that her body was about to die, but that it couldn't because her spirit was not yet ready. She would say: 'I'm going to cross over.' She said this more than once. Sometimes her spirit would be ready but not her body. She explained that once body and spirit would arrive at the threshold together, only then it would happen. She made it quite clear that she kept approaching the threshold, but then had to come back because either her spirit or her body wasn't ready. She described it so beautifully. It was so fascinating; both had to be ready at the same time. She was very calm about it, very thoughtful, and she died very peacefully.

Volunteer Tina talks about one resident:

We had a gentleman who always used to sit in a chair, but then he wanted to lie in bed. He was dying. Now and then he would lift himself up and reach for something, and said loud and clear: 'I want to get up, I want to go up there.' His family were there and they thought that he wanted to sit up in bed, but we were convinced he meant that 'up there' was somewhere beyond this world. He said it with such conviction and then he would lie down again, very calmly. We saw it differently than the family because when he was lying back and not sitting up, he was so calm. He wasn't as restless. He really was in an altered state of consciousness. He died a short time later.

Volunteer Josje about a resident:

Occasionally she was awake and was able to talk, and she would say that she was living in two worlds. Sometimes she saw things that I couldn't see, like a cat. She described in great detail how she saw it in a painting in her room. I thought: okay, you could see a cat in there. But what I found most interesting was when she talked about her husband who had already passed on. He was a Christian and was now somewhere beautiful where she wanted to be as well. Yet here she was, still in the hospice. Sometimes a good friend would visit and this meant she couldn't possibly leave yet! I asked her: 'Why don't you decide where you would really rather be?' She told me she just couldn't make up her mind. Something was still keeping her here.

Nurse Cocky tells us about someone who found himself in different realities:

This was such a wondrous situation. This man was in such poor condition and obviously dying, that I thought he would die within a couple of hours. He wasn't old, only 64, and had four beautiful children, who never left his side. They stayed with him in his room for two days. He would fall asleep, and then if he heard some music he would rally and say: 'Lovely', then he would fade away again. Whenever one of his children said something nice, he would look up and then fade away again. You could see and feel when he was in another world. We see it quite often, I've seen it myself. They are somewhere else for a short while and then they come back. You can see it in their eyes. Sort of looking, but not seeing. They look through you. The whole atmosphere changes, and when it does there is peace. It becomes serene, beautiful, it feels so nice. An absence of pain. A withdrawal from the world and all its problems, all its hassles. I find it lovely to see, and it leaves such an impression on me every time.

Supervisor Suzanne:

One of our volunteers was keeping watch with a resident when I walked into the room. I was standing behind the volunteer and looked at the sick and dying man. Then it seemed as though there were sparkles above him, all sparkles. I say 'sparkles', but it was something I really can't describe. It was so incredibly beautiful all I could do was stand and look. This gentleman had been dying for two weeks, but sometimes he really acted as though he were in heaven. Hilly, who plays harp at the hospice, had noticed it too. She told me about the first time that he was so far away. What really struck me about that day was the smell in his room. It changed the very first time he went 'heavenwards'. This man always had a very strong smell of urine and faeces around him, so we did our best to always keep his room fresh: with special perfume sprays, scented oil lamps and other air fresheners. We couldn't even keep his door open because the smell was so strong. The first Friday we noticed something was different about him, I walked into the room and the smell was gone. It smelt lovely.

What really struck me was that when he 'came back to earth' late on the Friday night and I went to work at the hospice the next morning, the old smell was back. It was so impressive! We had to use all the air fresheners again. Later on, the Friday before he died, two weeks after it happened for the first time, it smelt lovely again. Anyway, the unpleasant smell had become softer and milder in those two weeks, although he still had the problems with urine and faeces. And yes, I have an excellent sense of smell – it's my number one sense. It was when it smelled lovely that I saw those 'sparkles'. The following afternoon, he died.

Music therapist Hilly tells us about her observations:

When I'm playing the harp for people going through their final phase I can often clearly see how they go in and out of their bodies. It's an energetic perception, not in colours, but rather where the body's energy is centred. I sometimes see this movement in and out of their bodies directly and sometimes I perceive it through the reflection of my music. Later, when I write down and look at what I have done musically, I can sometimes see a back-and-forth movement. For instance, when I've made a somewhat strange alternation between small rhythmic pieces and other, much freer pieces, such as in a Gregorian chant where you are free in your movements. So it becomes a musical reflection of energetic experience. Sometimes I'm conscious of what I'm doing, and other times I only realise what I've done sometime later. Of course I'm conscious of what I'm playing, but that 'me' is not really there. It is performed from a kind of unity of consciousness. At that moment, the barrier between me and the other person is less distinct than it was when I came into the room. Together we enter an altered state of consciousness that predominates, but meanwhile the world as we normally perceive it is ever present. It's like subtitles. It doesn't disappear. It's still there but isn't intrusive. It's often accompanied by an atmosphere of calmness, peacefulness.

54

On two or three occasions I have distinctly noticed that people, who are only barely connected to their bodies, reconnect so deeply within their bodies while the music is playing. In every instance, the person died shortly afterwards. I interpreted that as a profound, perhaps the most profound incarnation of their lives. It's as though they have to say a very intense farewell to their bodies right down to the tips of their toes before they can leave their bodies.

LIGHT

—————⟫⟩⬦⟨⟪—————

"Light is the global symbol of divinity, of the spiritual element which flowed through the All after the primordial chaos of darkness and showed its boundaries to the shadows."[11] Light plays a vital role in almost every religious or mystic tradition. Most initiation ceremonies involve the idea of ascending to or into the light. In Buddhism, light represents the understanding of the truth and overcoming the material world on the path towards absolute reality. In Hinduism, light is a metaphor for wisdom. People who meditate regularly are able to enter a state of consciousness where they experience light and in which they connect to its main qualities, such as compassion and a universal, infinite love.

Those people who have had a near-death experience speak, almost without exception, about experiencing the light. They describe it as being warm, loving, immensely peaceful, and full of compassion and acceptance. They feel as though they are being drawn towards it. They often see light at the end of a tunnel, a light that is brighter and more powerful the further down the tunnel they travel.

I look into the Darkness.
In it there arises Light -
Living Light!
Who is this Light in the Darkness?

---

[11] Hans Biedermann (1991). *Symbolen. Historisch-culturele symbolen van A tot Z*. Utrecht: Het Spectrum.

It is I myself in my reality.
This reality of the I
Enters not into my earthly life;
I am but a picture of it.
But I shall find it again
When with good will for the spirit
I shall have passed through the Gate of Death.[12]

These experiences also occur on the deathbed, as we saw in Pauline's story for example. On the day before she died, Pauline's mother said: 'Pauline, please, never be afraid of dying. I saw a beautiful light and I was going towards it … it was so peaceful and it was so hard for me to come back.' Those who are dying report experiences with light less often, but it is obvious that these have an enormous impact on those involved. A profound feeling of peace and the absence of the fear of death experienced by the dying makes a lasting impression on those who are honoured to witness such an experience. Volunteer Jeannie, who told of her experiences earlier, greatly values her experiences with the light: 'How do I look back at what happened? I'm still incredibly grateful and am convinced that it exists. It's hard to go back into that experience but I felt it so strongly that when I read or hear about it, I think: yes, it's there.'

Volunteer Annelies tells us about a resident who experienced the light:

I remember someone who, just before she died, kept looking to her left, while I was sitting on her right. I asked her: 'Are you turning away? Would you like me to sit somewhere else?' A smile would often appear on her face and she said: 'I just see light, beautiful light.' I plucked up the courage to ask her if she could see any colours too. 'No,' she replied, 'I can't see any colours, I just see light, light.' She died in this position, turned towards her left, and while performing the after death care, I left her like that.

Hilly, music therapist:

I had some profound experiences when my mother was dying. During her last few hours, I had the feeling that I was travelling a long way with

---

[12] Rudolf Steiner, founder of Anthroposophy.

her. By then she was no longer conscious, but so much was happening, and I knew just how far I could travel with her and when I had to stop. This could have had something to do with the fact that, as a three year-old, I had a near-death experience in a dream. That's what it reminded me of. I could travel a long way with her but I knew, both as a child and by my mother's deathbed, that this was the line. This far and no further. A very strong threshold experience. After my mother died, I saw her surrounded by so much light and she had a look of intense peace on her face. It was amazing how much light there was.

Volunteer Anita:

Once I was sitting in a room where someone had died six hours before. While I was sitting there quietly, I saw a brilliant white light all around him. At first you think it's all in your imagination, but I just accepted it. It was such a special experience, seeing that abundance of light surrounding him. I'm still touched even talking about it now. I just sat there, thinking: maybe I can do something, just be here or help in some way. As I sat there, I felt very humble. Everything was already being taken care of, you see, there was nothing for me to do. This kind of care is far greater than anything I could imagine, a far greater intelligence is taking care of the deceased. Oh yes, it was a special experience. It affected me so much. I feel even more humble now. We can only do so much. We do a wonderful job, but you mustn't overestimate yourself, or try to make yourself important or try to do more than you are capable of. It humbles you.

DOGS, CATS
AND BIRDS

Animals seem to have a sense that gives them information before we humans receive it. In his book Dogs That Know When Their Owners Are Coming Home, Rupert Sheldrake analysed 2,500 instances of inexplicable behaviour in animals. He distinguishes between three major areas: telepathy, sense of direction (animals who can make their way home from places many miles away) and premonitions. We have also heard those dramatic stories about animals that have anticipated natural disasters and fled from the threatened areas. Most of us still have the horrific images of the tsunami engraved on our minds, which struck at the end of 2004. Many animals knew they had to flee to safety. One hour before the disaster, workers at a safari park noticed that elephants were leaving and that the bats were acting strangely. There are many stories about dogs who bark and cats who meow for no apparent reason. So it is hardly surprising that animals exhibit this super-sensitivity at the very moment that their owners die.

Volunteer Lisette talks about her father's death in the hospice where she works:

> The two dogs were lying on the floor. The younger dog stood up, started to lick my father's hand and pushed its nose into my father's palm. It pushed with its nose as if to say: 'I feel you and this is my hug for you.'

61

After a quarter of an hour, the other dog also stood up and began to howl. As soon as it has licked the top of his hands, my father died.

Volunteer Tina:

We had a lady staying with us with a small dog, which always sat on her bed and was very aggressive towards us. We weren't allowed to change the bed because it would go crazy. Then the day before she died, the dog got off the bed and jumped into my colleague's lap. It had never done that before because it didn't like strangers. It was as though the dog was distancing itself, and it never got back on the bed. The lady died shortly afterwards. It was the dog's way of saying farewell: I'm no longer with you, I'm on my own.

I also had a remarkable experience that might not quite fit in here, but I really want to share it with you. It's Christmas in 2005 and I'm the supervisor on call in the hospice. In the early morning on Christmas Day I wake up before the alarm goes off, I doze off again and have a dream. I'm holding a large, white cat in my arms. I'm cradling this long-haired cat and humming softly as though it were a baby. While wandering along, I occasionally look down lovingly at it. Suddenly, the cat leaps out of my arms. I look everywhere, but it's gone. It seems to have disappeared behind a veil of mist. Then the alarm goes off and I wake up. While eating my breakfast, I keep getting a flash of awareness that something important has happened but I can't put my finger on it. When I arrive at the hospice that morning, I know straight away that our resident Nel has died. A tiny, working-class lady with a full head of white hair. For the two months she was with us, she loved to sit in her chair by the window surrounded by all her favourite things. There were little hand-made witches and small embroidered pictures hanging on her wall. She did go back home for a short time to say her farewells, but then she came back here and never left her bed again. She was so tired and could feel her strength waning. Did she know she was going to die? For all those weeks when Nel was with us and we had the privilege to look after her, a big, white long-haired toy cat lay on her bed. When the funeral attendant took Nel's body the next day, the cat went into the coffin with her.

Birds are traditionally associated with death and for good reason. Flying symbolises escaping the physical limitations of our earthly lives and the ascent of the spirit to heaven. This is why birds are often seen as a sign of approaching death. Every culture has its own harbinger of death, such as black horses, black dogs and black butterflies, but birds are used in almost every culture. Ravens, owls, the white cockatoo and especially the crow, but also troupials (a family of songbirds which usually have black feathers, such as blackbirds, cowbirds and starlings) appear in worldly myths and folklore about dying and death. Black is the symbolic colour of the absolute (and in that sense is similar to its counterpart white) and depth psychologists consider it to be the colour of total unconsciousness, to be plunged into the dark, grief, in the darkness.[13]

Two fascinating examples of birds acting as messengers announcing approaching death.

Volunteer Diny tells us about the evening her husband died:

> Our neighbours are from Suriname and they said they kept seeing a blackbird flying around outside that evening. We thought that it was a bit strange. I called my sister-in-law in Sicily and asked her: 'There was a blackbird in our garden, have you any idea what that could mean?' 'Yes,' she answered, 'it will have come to collect the soul.' She was very sure about it. We delivered the after death care and at 2am everything was ready. Next morning, my daughter went home and my granddaughter told her: 'Mum, I woke up last night and there was a crow sitting outside my window, and it was cawing so loudly'. The other two grandchildren had also woken up, and they heard it too.

It isn't just loved ones who seem to be prepared in this manner, the dying can have such an experience too.

Simone, hospice supervisor, about her father:

Yes, my father saw crows. Actually before anybody had any idea that he was going to die. His nurse was deeply shocked. The people around him apparently found it more frightening than he did, because when

---

[13] Hans Biedermann (1991). *Symbolen. Historisch-culturele symbolen van A tot Z.* Utrecht: Het Spectrum.

I asked the nurse afterwards: 'Oh, was he afraid too?' it turned out he wasn't. He wasn't frightened, he just observed it: 'there are crows in the corner.'

A PRESENCE IS FELT IN THE ROOM FOR SOME TIME AFTER DEATH

Sometimes hospice caregivers sense a presence in the room after someone has died. They feel as though someone is still there. Sometimes it stops hospice caregivers from performing the after care for the deceased because they feel that they would be intruding in a process that was still going on. According to hospice caregivers, this process can take anything from a few moments to several days, and which gradually lessens in intensity. Earlier, we read the personal experience of Floortje, who could feel her husband's energy right up till the time he was buried. This presence after death is tangible by the atmosphere in the room. Those who are closest often talk about a warm, loving atmosphere. As volunteer in a hospice, I myself also had an experience with one of our residents who had been hovering between life and death for several days. As soon as she drew her last breath, I saw this gentle, loving smile on her face and the room was full of love, peace and calm. It was a feeling I will never forget. However, some presences felt after death are not so pleasant.

Nurse Mieke tells us that the atmosphere in the rooms of the dying can vary a great deal:

With some people it is very eerie, while for others it's peaceful, very pleasant, very warm. Sometimes I just don't want to go into the room of a resident who has died, something just feels wrong in there. Yet I can sit by the bedside of others for hours. But sometimes something stops me from going in and I just have to turn back.

Volunteer Liesbeth talks about a disturbing experience she had, this time just after the death of a resident:

We had a resident who was in a very bad way but still with us. The nurse had just been in his room and told me: 'Something doesn't feel right, it really is a bit nasty. You go in and see how you feel.' I said: 'Alright, but I'll leave the door open.' I was wary, and walked in. I just stood there and all of a sudden my whole body started to shiver. I walked past the bed to the door and when I was about to open it, I felt: I have to get out, get out, get out. I can't really put it into words but I was petrified. I glanced at the man and had such a shock, it was as though I was looking at the devil lying in bed. I walked out, shaking with fear, my heart was racing. The nurse could see I was in a bad way, that I needed to catch my breath. It was such an intense experience. The image of the man with that devilish expression. So much malice. I am very down to earth and knew that the evil energy didn't come from me. I just couldn't go back into that room. Then Ad arrived, we were on duty together that day. We told him what had happened and he went inside, but he couldn't sense anything wrong, nothing at all. Later on, the nurse burnt some sage to purify the room.

Some people are very sensitive to energies and can pick them up all too easily. 'It was as if the devil was lying there in that bed', Liesbeth told us. It may sound strange but sometimes there do seem to be some powerful and inexplicable forces present around a deathbed. Forces beyond our control which seem to bear witness to evil or some kind of possession. This man's daughter admitted later that her father had had many enemies when he was alive.

Anyway, it is important that hospice caregivers take themselves seriously and not ignore these kinds of experiences, whether they are pleasant or unpleasant.

Nurse Willy had such an experience and tells us how she dealt with it:

> One experience that affected me a great deal concerned a young man
> with a brain tumour, who used to be a TV director. Lots of young
> people came to visit him. He was actually in a coma and his death
> followed quite soon after. He had wanted to be taken away after his
> death and laid out at home. I went into his room, but had the feeling
> that I shouldn't clean or do anything else yet. I left and went to see
> our psychosocial worker and told her how I felt, that the man's spirit
> was still there. Then she said, and this was an enormous help: 'What
> do you want to do?' I told her that I wanted to say goodbye to him.
> She helped me to do it. Together we looked for a poem and went into
> his room. I lit some candles, placed a flower by his photo and read out
> the poem, just the two of us. Then it felt right. I don't think anyone
> else felt like that, but I certainly did.

Willy describes doing something that really worked for her. Rituals
like these allow us to take a moment to be still, before we can move on.
All three hospices have a quiet room, which is the perfect place to be
when the staff have come off duty or need to work through an intense
experience. Sometimes, residents' rooms have to be purified so that
negative energies don't linger. Sage cleanses and purifies the energies
in a room and burning it can serve as a ritual. To cleanse using sage,
place the dried leaves or stems in a bowl, or a shell used especially for
this purpose. If you douse the fire by blowing gently, you will create
smoke. This smoke is cleansing and can be spread around using the
hands or a feather to dissipate any negative energies.

Hilly, music therapist:

> When someone has just passed away, I can feel a presence when I'm in
> their room. Once, when a presence was particularly strong, I shared
> the experience with a nurse. She could feel it too. Some people leave
> very quickly, others linger.

In the chapter 'After death care experiences', you can read about
more experiences of hospice caregivers in respect of the presence of
subtle energies, 'tuning in' and caring for the deceased.

POETRY, PROSE
AND HYMNS

Thing is a Bible in almost every room in the hospices. If not, you are sure to find bibles, journals, or other religious writings in the quiet rooms. Sometimes volunteers ask if the residents would like them to read for them. Sometimes the residents themselves will ask. It's a lovely way to spend time together. Psalm 130 for example, often tends to offer comfort during the final stage and will sometimes be read over and over.

Suzanne also has this experience:

> Oh yes, I remember a gentleman who always wanted to hear readings from the Bible. He even asked me, even though I don't understand the stories and I'm not a very good reader. He just wanted to hear them. He enjoyed it and it comforted him. He was a very nervous man, he just wanted to smoke and drink whisky but when we read him the psalms, he would calm down. It was so important to him! But it was almost unnatural: I mean, sure, having a psalm read to you once is fine, but he wanted to hear it for 24 hours straight! If we just sat quietly with him, he would become restless, but if we read to him, he became calm.

Lisette talks about a resident who leaned towards Buddhism, and for whom singing Buddhist mantras offered guidance:

This lady told me: 'I'm standing in front of the gates but I daren't go in. I'm afraid.' Then she held my hand tightly. 'I don't dare take that last step yet, I just don't.' She really wasn't able to die. This went on for three or four days. She played her mantras and sang along and whoever was on duty, including me, tried to join in. Suddenly she would say: 'That's enough' and she wanted to listen to a different one. She kept saying: 'I mustn't panic', because she would then take the panic with her through the transition. Buddhists must try to be as calm as possible and she wasn't that calm yet. She was very aware of that.

Annelies, volunteer:

> There was a lady with us and every time I'd pop in to check that she was still alive, even though we had agreed to leave her alone more so she could have the chance to retreat into herself. I looked round the door and she suddenly opened her eyes. She beckoned me and asked me to sing Psalm 34 with her. All sorts of things went through my mind: I can't sing, I don't know Psalm 34, where can I find it ... but I also couldn't leave her. I held her hand and said: 'I am a Catholic, I don't know Psalm 34, but I can say the Lord's Prayer with you.' She moved her head which I took as a 'yes', so we said the Lord's Prayer together. She died shortly afterwards.

All sorts of things went through Annelies' mind. She didn't know the psalm, she didn't know where to find a prayer book, but she thought: I can't just walk away. The lady had chosen that very moment. Not Annelies, but the moment, and Annelies knew that she had to stay with that moment. Such presence of mind. Because she didn't know the psalm, she offered to pray. She also couldn't remember all of the Lord's Prayer: 'I did leave out a few bits, but I know Our Lord wouldn't mind. I prayed with her.' Although there were things missing, Annelies did what was needed in the moment.

Sometimes hospice caregivers are asked to pray with the dying. For some of them, like Annelies, it isn't a problem, but for others who are not brought up that way it can be a dilemma. Respect for their own limitations is important for every hospice worker. If a volunteer can't or won't accede to such a request, then there will probably be a fellow volunteer in the hospice who can pray with the resident. Of course, their own priest, vicar, or spiritual counsellor can be invited to be at the bedside of the dying.

In the middle of the night, nurse Wilma found a way to meet a request,
although not quite completely:

> One of our ladies called for me in the middle of the night. She was very
> restless. 'What's wrong?' I asked her, and she replied: 'It just doesn't
> feel right.' 'How can I help?' 'Would you say a Hail Mary with me?'
> I answered: 'I don't know how, but I can pray with you. Would you
> like that? The Lord's Prayer?' I lit a candle and we prayed. Then she
> said: 'That was lovely.' The room felt calm and peaceful. She died soon
> afterwards, although she wasn't really in such a bad way at that time.

Faith can often provide great comfort, but for some it can give rise
to fear and tension on their deathbed.

Volunteer Tini explained how faith can cause fear:

> I have indeed noticed that religious people who are about to die start
> worrying about whether or not they will be forgiven. So yes, they start
> thinking back to things they have done. I've had a whole conversation
> with someone about why he would go to hell, or at least not receive
> God's mercy. Eventually I said: 'You're thinking like a human being,
> but God isn't human. He is much more loving than we are with each
> other. Why would he punish you because you went to the cinema?
> That's human punishment, it's not divine.' We talked about it a lot.
> At a certain moment he found Forgiveness. That's how he put it. In
> the last week before he died he was calm, the battle was over. I think
> there's always a kind of battle. Yes, a battle to come to terms with how
> they have lived their lives.

Volunteer Cok:

> People often want you to read to them. Sometimes they have a book
> by the bed and sometimes, when you take over a shift, you'll be told
> that this resident or that resident has asked to be read to. You can see
> how much it comforts them, and when it offers comfort it's a beautiful
> thing. Sometimes people have lived very religious lives and this can
> make them rather tense on their deathbed. I find that one of the most
> painful things. I was once with a lady who was so frightened. She kept
> saying that she was sure she wasn't good enough to go to heaven. I
> told her: 'You remind me so much of my granny...' She had died thirty

years ago and was very religious. Towards the end she was suffering from dementia, but then she would suddenly ask her children: "Go and get my coat." "Why do you want your coat?" they would ask. And she would say: "Jesus is coming to collect me, I have to be ready." I told the lady this story. I could see her face relax somewhat and she fell asleep peacefully. A lovely example of saying the right thing at the right time, although I am usually very reserved.

It doesn't always have to be the Bible that residents want to be read to from. Sometimes they have a favourite book of their own, or there's something in the hospice library. Stories and poems by Toon Tellegen, stories and fairytales on the threshold between life and death or various works of poetry are all beautiful examples.

Volunteer Tini:

One lady never wanted to talk about the fact that she was going to die, even though I was very close to her. She always let me read to her, and then she would go quiet and say 'Thank you.' I read to her from a book of fairy tales and also from the Bible, about love, Corinthians 13, I believe it was. She used to love that and it made her happy, very happy. She's the one who showed me that everyone dies in their own way.

She wouldn't talk about dying. She wasn't going to die and didn't want to hear about it. When I was about to go on holiday, I said gently: 'I just wanted to say goodbye.' She looked so surprised and didn't feel the need to say our goodbyes. I thought she knew best and I really think she did, but she wouldn't admit it. She did indeed die the evening before I came back from holiday. Yes, I knew it would happen. I felt that I had to say goodbye to her, even though it would make her sad. Not just because she had to say goodbye to me, but also because she would soon be saying goodbye to life itself. People do it in their own way, depending on how they have lived. I sincerely believe that.

Volunteer Helen:

Before people start to fade away, you know what they're like, for example whether or not they like to be read to. One lady had a book by her bed that she found very depressing. She told me: 'I'm actually a very positive sort of person.' She was also very patient. The end was very difficult, it took a long time before she died. I looked for a book to cheer her up, all about the lovely, positive things in life. She found that grief and suffering weighed her down. She saw and wanted only positive things, because that's how she approached life. It was beautiful to see the way she dealt with it. I would read to her and now and then she would fall asleep. At one point she was very far away but I carried on reading, because I thought that she might still be able to hear me. And for me it was nice too. It left a huge impression on me.

Suzanne, supervisor:

We had a gentleman who first used to always sit in his chair, but then wanted to lie in bed. He was slipping further away and spent most of the time sleeping. Then he suddenly got up and started looking amongst his CDs for one in particular. It took him a long time because he was very weak. Then he wanted to listen to the same CD over and over again, an album by Sting. He died two days later. It was such an enormous change, going from that deep sleep to wanting to listen to music.

It's usually religious people who gain the most comfort from the singing of songs.

Volunteer Anke:

They often sing to themselves. Sometimes they tell me a line from a song and if I know it, I will sing some of it for them. Then they feel a sense of relief; 'Yes, that's the one.' It comforts them. You can see it in their eyes and on their faces. If I had to sum up what I am seeing in one word, I would call it acceptance.

THE DESIRE FOR RECONCILIATION

The desire for reconciliation is one example of a final meaning ELE. As people are nearing the end of their lives they take stock of those lives. This can awaken a desire for reconciliation and a need to complete unfinished business. Resolving these issues can relieve existential anxiety and unease and allows the dying to prepare spiritually for the approaching death.

Volunteer Lisette about rounding off one's life:

> I came across something like this with a lady from the South of Rotterdam. All she had was the one son. This son needed care and depended on assisted-living facilities. There came a time when she had to tell him that he would have to take care of himself from now on. She told him everything he needed to know so that he could carry on without her. When she had finished, she went to see all her old neighbours to say goodbye. You could see that she was ready to go. Before then she always wanted to sit in the same chair, but now she wanted to get into bed, and she never left it again.

A similar experience is told by Simone, supervisor:

> A lady who had not been with us for very long had an autistic son.
> There was a very close bond between mother and son. At one point
> she gave him a lecture: what he should do to cope and that he had to
> take care of himself; at this time there was no indication that she was
> going to die. However, shortly after this she passed away. She knew
> more than we did. She just needed to get these things done. For me,
> this kind of thing is a sign that there probably isn't much time left.

Sometimes it's enough for people to express their regrets.

*Volunteer Gon talks about her first ELE, which happened when she was
still working in a hospital:*

> I was working as a physiotherapist in the hospital, when I had an
> experience with a patient, which made a big impression on me. He was
> a union leader. In those days we would use the chest clapping technique
> to drain mucus. It was awful for everyone involved, but people were
> too weak to cough up the mucus by themselves. This man called for
> me and I clapped his chest to loosen up the mucus. It seemed that he
> was full of regrets that he had spent his life either working or in bars,
> and had neglected his wife and children. He was a lovely man, full of
> life, bright, witty and kind. When I had finished, I left him but fifteen
> minutes later I was called back, because he was so short of breath. I
> looked at him and thought: I can't do this, he's too weak. While I was
> sitting there with him, he died. I couldn't believe it. Someone who,
> just a quarter of an hour before, had been so lively, fully conscious,
> yes, perfectly aware. It left a deep impression on me. I felt sure that I
> had given this patient relief for the last half an hour, even if it was only
> physical relief. And maybe it had also done him good to express his
> regrets about what he had left behind, for his wife and children. So, I
> mean ... I was there just at the right time.

When it comes to taking stock of their lives, the dying are sometimes not able to speak about it with the people directly involved. The
emotional bond and the emotional pain can be just too great.

A volunteer recognises the need to heal rifts through a personal experi-
ence with her family-in-law:

> In the last week when he [father-in-law] was in a very 'bad way' in the
> hospital, I spent a lot of time at his bedside with my mother-in-law,
> supporting her as well. She couldn't see that he was 'in a bad way': he
> was in the hospital and they were going to make him better. My father-
> in-law noticed this and started to talk to me a lot. He was really mean
> to my mother-in-law, I could see that it was his way of pulling away
> from her and creating some distance. At the same time I could see
> that he needed to heal rifts. He was never a man to dwell on sorrow
> or pain, but just then I found myself listening to all kinds of personal
> memories about what happened between him and his own parents,
> things he had found difficult to deal with. He also talked about his deep
> sorrow for a child who died two days after birth. My mother-in-law said
> 'Oh, why do you want to rake that all up now?' I told her: 'He can tell
> me, it's important for him.' He also talked about a row he'd had with
> his brother, and how much it hurt him that he had never reconciled
> with him, and how afraid he was that the same thing would happen
> to his two sons. Actually he was giving a sort of warning: 'Don't wait
> too long.' So perhaps he wanted to break the pattern by talking about
> his own pain. This way he was able to make amends with his family.

Supervisor Simone tells us of an intense and profound experience,
which was also healing, especially for a resident's partner. She told me:
'You are in a kind of flow, where everything falls into place and finds
its own level. You can't force it to happen. It only happens when you
are willing to be open to it. It's a matter of being receptive and going
along with it, to move with the impulses. The less I actually think about
it, the easier it flows.' This is her story:

> We had admitted a gentleman who came from Amsterdam. His
> partner, Jos, lived in Rotterdam so that's why he came to stay with us
> in the hospice. He was Portuguese, an older man who had no friends
> at all. He was lonely and very ill. When he arrived at the hospice, he
> decided to close his eyes, and we just couldn't reach him. Neither could
> his partner Jos, who had been taking care of him in Amsterdam. Jos
> went home that same afternoon without having spoken to his friend,
> which appeared to be a huge burden for him. 'I've let him down', he said.

This gentleman stayed with us for two weeks. For the first week, he kept his eyes tightly shut and wouldn't communicate with us at all. In the second week, we could see that he was getting weaker. His friend Jos came every day and stayed by his bedside till 5 o'clock. One day, Jos came to me to tell his story and asked: 'How long will this go on?' Then I said: 'You know what, let's go and see him together.' We stood by the bed, and Jos expressed his feelings of guilt again for not speaking to his friend again, how hard he was finding it and how sad he was. He was also troubled that his friend was disappointed in life. It was a long story. Then he sat on the bed and gently stroked his friend's head; suddenly his eyes opened. It was a truly magical moment. I stopped what I was doing and stood back. I knew I mustn't intrude. Jos told him what a good friend he'd been and that he'd taught him so much. His friend's eyes stayed open. He was trying to do something with his hand, but didn't have the strength. He couldn't speak, but they looked deeply into each other's eyes. This went on for about ten minutes. Then his eyes slowly closed, and he died. It was an extraordinary moment. It was so important to Jos that he was able to say what he did, and I had the feeling that his friend could hear him. So he died, with someone at his bedside who was telling him how special he was. By then it was 5.30. It occurred to me: normally Jos would have left by then, he never stayed after 5 o'clock. Something had helped to let him stay longer. It was a kind of miracle. I held my breath for so long, I thought my heart would stop. And yes, I was witness to it all. That's what I told Jos: 'No one will believe it when you tell them, but I saw it.' It was so special. Incredibly moving. Someone who had kept his eyes shut for two weeks, then made contact again just at the final moment.

This experience is a lovely example of how circumstances can sometimes rise above themselves so that everything falls into place, that we can observe a kind of order, and that there is a significance to everything that happens when someone dies, no matter how incomprehensible it might seem to us. Apparently, what is most essential is not to orchestrate or organise. The most essential things will simply happen.

Sometimes families struggle with unfinished business, or because there's something they still want to say. The following example from volunteer Josje shows us that it doesn't have to happen straight away, there can be other ways of dealing with it. In the situation described here, a daughter opens her heart to Josje and releases herself from the negative emotions and pain about her mother.

Josje:

One time, while I was on night duty, the daughter of one of our residents came to see me. She still had things she needed to say to her mother and asked me if she could go and talk to her about it. I found it hard to answer her, but I said: 'If you could share it here with us first, perhaps you'll feel different when you go in to see your mother.' And she took that opportunity. She felt relieved, which felt good to her. Then she went in to see her mother, who died shortly afterwards, at a moment when her daughter had briefly left the room again.

As the moment of her death was approaching, I could sense something: I was with another resident, but knew I had to go to her. I went to her and I stayed. She died while I was with her. Her daughter came in shortly afterwards. She told me that because she had been able to pour out her heart she went into her mother's room in a different frame of mind, and it had felt right. And that it was alright that she hadn't been there when her mother actually died, and that she was happy that I had been there. I guess I had acted as a kind of intermediary.

Nurse Wilma talks about the completion and closure of life:

Sometimes, we have very young people who say that they feel so torn up inside. They actually do want to go to the people they have already lost, to the afterlife, but have children to leave behind. This is something I find really difficult. How can they find closure? People feel that they are still needed. Sometimes, it's the children that really surprise you. We had a lady here who had a six month old baby and a little boy of about five. Her illness was progressing very quickly and she was so angry. She was so full of rage and turmoil. I found it hard to talk to her because she was resisting so fiercely, she thought it was so unfair. It was hard for me too. I was standing in the corridor and thought, I wish I could get inspiration from above ... how can I help her? Her resistance was only getting worse. Anger, hostility and obstinacy. Then her little boy wandered innocently into the room, so disarming. He sat on his Mum's bed and then something happened. Something actually happened. I could see all her hostility melting away, replaced by sorrow. I could see the effect that little boy had on his mother ... and sometimes yes, it's almost too much. Now her resistance had been broken, she could prepare herself for death, say

79

goodbye to the two little children who were at her bedside until the last moment. At one point I could see that her hostility towards her husband had melted too. I was there when she died and it's a moment I'll never forget. I told her: 'Saskia, it will be alright, you can go, you can go ... your husband and the little ones will cope. They really will.' And within five minutes, she died. She looked at me, relaxed a little, and could just let it go.

Coming to terms with the life as it was lived seems to be, as we discussed earlier, an autonomous aspect of our life process, or maybe even the autonomous life process itself. That sometimes things happen outside our personal control is illustrated by Nurse Cocky's experience. It's amazing what can happen in the final stages when the soul takes over from personality. When life is lived until it's done.

Cocky:

A very special process was that of an extraordinary lady who didn't want anyone at her bedside. She didn't want to see her children any more, which was so awful for them. You could see adult men in tears, aimlessly walking through the corridors because they couldn't go in to see her. The next day she said to me: 'Do you get it? I've said goodbye to my children and then I don't die ...' She was a very intelligent, educated woman who had studied chemistry. So this was how she thought about it. But this was only the beginning of the process she was about to go through with her children. They were quite remarkable too: one a follower of the Hare Krishna, another of the Bhagwan. Anyway, she didn't want to see anyone, even though it was so difficult for her, but, she'd said it and that was that. Meanwhile she became more and more sick.

Then, when a temporary staff member mistakenly let her daughter into the room following some miscommunication, the situation changed. You could see that sometimes it's a good thing when someone just doesn't know, and things can just happen. Suddenly other things were possible and she wanted to see her children again. They came in one by one to say goodbye. It turned out that this lady had always found it difficult to show her feelings, especially to her children. Now she could. One son stroked her arm and said: 'Mum, this is what you've always wanted.' It was so intense. It's incredible how much can happen in the final stages, isn't it. And if we had chosen euthanasia, then none of these things could have happened. Amazing.

Reconcilement is not just about tying up loose ends with other people. Reconcilement is also about acceptance of the life as it was lived. It's always the dying who pass final judgement when weighing up their lives, and for the religious, this means asking for God's mercy.

Nurse Willy tells us that religious people are often the most afraid:

For those who are strictly Reformed and who have lived their life with a God who judges you, and who also must give you his blessings before you can enter the gates of heaven, this is quite disturbing. They ask: 'Do you think I will still get there?' This really worries them. This is why we often call in the help of a minister or vicar who will then visit the hospice. Do these people also have visions and dreams? No, I've never seen it. Twice, we had a religious couple who visited us one after the other. First as visitors, then as residents. I remember that one of the ladies had great passivity; she lay waiting within herself and in tremendous loneliness. I never heard her or any of the others talk about visions or nice experiences, thoughts or hopes. No, they used to ask: 'Where will I end up?' and 'Have I been good?' When people are so religious, I want to tell them: 'I'm sure that God doesn't work that way.' But that just isn't possible. Someone who is eighty years old and believes in a God who judges everything he or she has done, finds this impossible to accept. They have to come to terms with their own lives by consulting with and talking to their own minister.

Faith can also offer strength to the believer. Volunteer Helen talks about a young religious man who had sorted out all practical matters in his life and was ready to go to God:

He was so very young, and so very sick. He assured me: 'Everything's arranged, all is well. The mourning card is ready, all that needs to be filled in is the date. It's all arranged and I know exactly where I'm going, the Lord has shown me everything.' So he had sorted his earthly business and he knew exactly where he was heading in the hereafter. He said: 'I know just where I'm going. I asked the Lord not to show me Hell, just Heaven'. Yes, he was expected and he sounded very content, for everything was ready and well and he felt that he could go.

It's not always possible to heal family rifts. But it is important for hospice caregivers to realise that they only accompany a person for a short distance on his or her life path and that they do not know the life history of that person.

Nurse Willy tells more about that:

> Quite regularly I see concrete examples of this. It was like that with a lady who had breast cancer. She had dreadful wounds and was in terrible pain. She had lost touch with two of her sons. When she realised that she wasn't going to recover, she wanted to see them. They were traced and came to see her. I understood from the sons that they wanted to respond to their mother's desire for them to come and say goodbye, but that was all they could do. Too much had been ruined in their life. But they knew it was important to their mother and it was something they could still do for her. They told me: 'We can't sit by her bed, that's asking too much.' Their mother couldn't talk about her feelings and was in a great deal of pain, but she said: 'I'm so glad I could see them one more time, it's good like this.' This was as much as could be expected, more wasn't possible.
>
> I also remember a resident who said: 'I want to die here on my own and I don't want anyone to know.' He had just one daughter. We respected his wishes. A couple of days later, a lady came to the front door and said: 'I'm Mr Van Santen's daughter and I read in the paper that he died here. I think it's awful that you didn't let me know. I explained to her that this was her father's wish and we had to respect it. I did make sure she was able to work through her grief, but it was very painful. It doesn't always work out well. No, it really doesn't. Not between parents and children either. Although I do have an example of a daughter who was abused by her father, but who could still find it in her heart to be there. He was a very selfish man, and so it was difficult to offer him adequate care. We only touch each other's lives for a brief time. There is a whole life story behind it and it isn't always possible to heal or to mend family rifts.

Sometimes experiences are so traumatic that they seem insurmountable. Hospice volunteer Ina tells us her personal story:

> I came to work in the hospice because I wasn't there when my father died. I didn't want to be there, it was a conscious decision. My father

was a violent man and I was still frightened. I was frightened that he would hurt me again. It was very hard having to make a decision like that. He kept looking at the door and asking my younger sister: 'Does Ina know, does Ina know?' But Ina never came, because Ina was much too scared. Looking back though, I felt terrible that I hadn't been there. It was really difficult. It preyed on my mind.

I made that decision then because I was simply left with no other choice. That much is certain. But then I started to listen deeply within: how it came about, how he came to be like that. I wrote down my father's life story after he died, by listening to him. He had left me a record, A German Requiem by Brahms and as soon as I heard the first notes, I cried like never before. 'It can't be, it just can't be.' I played the record again and again and thought: how can this be? That this man, this violent man, could appreciate such beautiful music? It just didn't fit. Through the musical notes, I began to tune into my father. I could almost feel him; then he started to 'talk'. I have no idea how that was even possible. It seemed that he was afraid to die. That's how I see him now, clinging to the bed. He had turned to religion and used to give money to the Church. He was afraid of dying, as if to say: I am being called to account. It must have been a tremendous struggle. Terrible.

After he died I felt a bit safer; there was no more physical fear. I had to go beyond my judgement about my father. So every time that he 'told' me something, I thought: yes, but ... and I felt like hitting and screaming, but every time I had to turn back: 'Ina, shut up, shut up.' Just until I could listen to it. It was a truly essential experience. I'm also extremely glad that I did it. That I kept going back until I could eventually reach the love I felt for him but that I no longer knew. Now I can say: 'Yes, I love that man.' And that still moves me.

Ina shows us how the violence of the past made it impossible to communicate with her father. After his death, she found the courage to go through a painful and difficult process of reconciliation. She was able to re-establish the connection with her father, by purifying it and ridding herself of all the negative feelings from the past. Ina was even able to rediscover the love that she had for her father. It was a healing process and a powerful story, which shows that it's never too late to try to find reconciliation.

UNEXPECTED LUCID
MOMENTS

People who are dying and with whom contact hasn't been possible for some time because they seem so far gone, totally withdrawn within themselves or comatose, appear to be capable of having unexpected lucid moments, in which they are able to say goodbye to their loved ones. I experienced this with Mrs. Kraaikamp, a resident who was both deaf and unable to speak. This called for a very special way of communicating. Metastases in her liver made her look very yellow. Perhaps she was always of slight build, but now she was just skin and bones and translucent like an angel. She had been 'unapproachable' for several days and seemed to be in another world altogether, when she suddenly opened her eyes and looked at her family one by one. Then her eyes seemed to drift away from everyone. Although it seemed physically impossible, she sat up, held her arms out wide, and a radiant smile spread over her face. Then she sank back into her pillows and died. Not only was I witness to an unexpected lucid moment in which she said goodbye to her loved ones, but looking at that radiant smile on her face, this was quite possibly also a vision in which she met other meaningful figures. This was one of my first experiences as a volunteer in the hospice and the seemingly boundless feeling of tranquillity and peace during that moment has stayed with me to this day.

Cynthia:

Sometimes people seem to have a revival. They have been sleeping a lot, and then there seem to be signs of improvement. There are many who have such a revival and then ask to see someone, who in such cases usually comes almost straight away. I remember a lady whose friend, with whom she'd had a falling out, came to see her. They talked together and then she faded away again. I've seen this on several occasions, that someone comes by with whom they speak or resolve their issues.

Nurse Mieke:

I've witnessed a couple of times that people would sit up completely straight, while this should have been physically impossible. For example someone who sat up with outstretched arms, then lay down again and died. It was as if there was a meeting of sorts. Or eyes that suddenly open and look at something, when those same eyes have been closed for such a long time.

Volunteer Tini talks about an experience with her husband who was in a coma:

He had drifted far away, but then all of a sudden he was able to say that everything was alright and that he was ready, in spite of all the struggle he went through. There was peace. It wasn't the dying that was hard for him, it was leaving us. He was lovely. He did it with such respect, not only considering himself, but considering us too.

This last example shows us how much it can mean for the family when a loved one who is dying has a lucid moment as a sign of saying farewell.

WAITING FOR THE ARRIVAL OR DEPARTURE OF FAMILY

It happens all too often that people wait with dying until a family member arrives at the bedside, or even wait with dying until everyone has left the room. It's as though, on the one hand, the dying have the ability to postpone the moment of passing and, on the other, are powerless in making the transition when their loved ones are there with them.

Nurse Mieke talks about this:

> Sometimes people keep waiting for someone and you think, why is it taking so long? People just can't seem to let go. One gentleman was taking a very long time in the final stage, but died as soon as his two brothers were there in his room. Then I wonder, is this a coincidence?, but I don't think it is. Yes, it's like something is keeping them here. And you often see people waiting for someone, so they can express something or resolve their issues.

> However, there are also people who wait until everyone leaves. That everyone is out of the room. Then I ask the family what the person was like when he or she was alive. How they coped with illnesses or how they overcame problems in their lives; if they wanted company or not. Did they like lots of visitors or did they hide in bed under the

blankets. The latter are usually the people who would rather die alone. Do people die as they have lived? Yes, oftentimes they do.

Volunteer Anke talks about people who wait until they have seen or talked with someone before dying:

People who realise: I can't go yet, I need to talk to my son or my daughter. I often see this. Yet it doesn't always work out that way of course. And then to see the intense grief when it can't be done and letting go becomes so difficult. That's what I put in the category of a 'dying emergency'. Real torment. That is truly suffering.

Diny:

A lady was constantly with her family, who at one point had all gone out to have a cup of coffee. I saw them sitting in the family room and I thought: I'll just go in and check on her. But directly afterwards something told me not to go in. A little while later, the nurse came by and said: 'Let's just pop in.' We found that the lady had just died. The nurse went to call the family in, but I stayed behind; there was one last sigh. That feeling that I shouldn't go in ... I don't know what it was. But soon thereafter, it was all over and she died alone. It's as though she needed to be alone.

The same thing happened with another lady. She was extremely ill, but her mind was still strong. The family often came to visit and that would cheer her up. Then at one point she said: 'No, you all go home, you don't have to stay.' She was given a hand and foot massage and I brought her a hot water bottle. She lay comfortably in her bed and when everyone had left, she died alone. As though she didn't want anyone to be with her. I believe that people want to die in their own way. Some want their whole family around them while others would rather be alone. The people I have just told you about are those who think: I'll just slip away when everyone's gone. The second lady, who said: 'Just go', was a very independent sort. As far as I could tell, it fit with the kind of person she was.

Diny talks about her own husband:

We knew and felt that it was coming. He was already on morphine and wasn't really with us. We knew but even so, it happened when we had just left him for a moment. My daughter had said: 'Mum, let's all eat here this evening. I know it will be noisy with all the children and grandchildren, but Dad likes it when we're all together. Then he'll hear that everything's alright.' So that's what we did. My son and I just popped out to get a lamp from another room, and when we got back we could feel the silence. My son went to his bedside to look but I said straight away: 'Call everyone in.' He had slipped away in that one minute when we weren't there. He must have thought: it's time now.

Supervisor Simone:

We once had a lady who said to us: 'I feel so awful, am I going to die?' She was perfectly lucid and aware, and there was no indication at all that this would happen. At the same time her friend arrived and wanted to say hello. We were busy determining whether she needed more medication. She didn't really want to see her friend because she was feeling so ill, so she said: 'I'm just going to have a nap.' I asked her: 'Can your friend still come in to say goodbye?' He did go in and then he left. She died half an hour later. That's one of those moments when you think, how can it be that you are just part of the flow when everything falls into place? That we are given the space? This man was so moved that he had been the last person to see her. She had been the last one to see his wife before she died. Layer upon layer which were hugely important to him. And in that half an hour before she died, she'd had a hug from a very close friend.

Volunteer Cok:

I had known this man for almost two years from my work in home care. At first I just visited occasionally, then more often. When he couldn't get out of bed anymore, I was there three times a week, so I was like part of the furniture. We talked about what he wanted to wear. It had to be a suit. But oh dear, he was so thin, he'd lost so much weight. He wanted me to wash and iron his shirt. He mentioned his socks: 'They won't be able to find them later.' I told him: 'Then I'll put them in your jacket pocket.' That's the kind of thing we did together.

He'd had a Christian upbringing, but in the course of his life he had let it lapse. But once he was confined to his bed he turned back to it. Every now and again he'd ask: 'Cok, do you ever pray?' and I would answer: 'Sure I do.' He said: 'I pray for you too, because the work you do is so demanding.' Then I said: 'If I pray for you, can I ask for anything special for you?' 'Well,' he replied, 'I'd like to stay a bit longer.'

Then he started to get worse and worse, and I was going on holiday. I had promised him that if I was anywhere near, I wanted to help with the last offices. He was so pleased. He told me: 'You're so neat, so at least I know I'll look my best.' While I was on holiday, he called all his children and grandchildren together. He had something to say to each of them. When he'd finished, he looked round and said: 'But someone's missing.' His daughter told him: 'But Dad, you know that Cok is on holiday and we can't call her.' He held out for ten more days. I really think that he had waited for me. When I saw him again, he was already near the end, his voice was very weak: 'I'm so glad you're back.' He lived on the second floor and could look out over the Amsterdam Rijn Canal in the distance and the railway line behind it. He kept looking outside and said: 'Look at that, just look at that.' So I asked: 'Do you mean the trains?' 'No.' 'The boats?' 'No,' he replied, 'Higher up.' All I could see was the blue sky so I said: 'I think you're looking at something that I can't see, so I think it might be almost time.' 'Yes,' he said, 'I think you're right.' He could feel that it was close. I sat with him for a while, then he put his hand to his mouth to call out to what he saw, but his voice had gone. He was so weak. It was very moving. I said: 'I'll be back tomorrow at about eleven o'clock.' Then he frowned and looked doubtful. I told him: 'Don't worry if that's too long, you don't have to wait for me. If you have to go, then have a good journey.' He nodded, and I left. His daughter was outside in the corridor, smoking a cigarette and I said: 'Stay near your father because he's looking over the threshold now and is seeing something we can't see, at what's coming.' But she replied: 'Oh I doubt it, he's often confused.' I'd been home for half an hour when she called: 'Dad has died.' Yes, I was afraid of that. It was a really special experience. He was so very close, and I had the privilege to share part of it with him.

It seems that the dying choose their moment of death more often than we realise. It's not unusual for the dying to wait for a distant relative or a close friend. Sometimes the reason to stay is a wedding anniversary

or a birthday, the arrival of a first grandchild, or an important milestone that must be reached. However impossible it might seem medically, the dying are able to summon enough vital energy. There are also stories of people who chose to die only when certain people were around them. Some relatives can suddenly have an irresistible urge to visit the dying, even if it's the middle of the night, or feel that they are being called back to the bedside when they have just gone out for a cup of tea. Volunteer Diny followed her instinct not to go into a resident's room at that moment and allowed her to die on her own. This can also be people's choice. They wait until everyone has left the room, and choose that moment to die. It's as though circumstances don't let us control them, but act autonomously and meaningful around the dying process, with the consequence that the right people are present when it matters most. That can be hard for closest family and friends when they have spent so long worrying and waiting by the bedside, and their loved one slips away when they have just left the room. They may feel hurt or guilty, because they feel they have let their partner, father or mother down at that crucial moment. It's good to remember that sometimes the dying need the freedom to die by themselves in peace and tranquillity. It can also be that the emotional bond between people is so strong and that letting go is so difficult, that they choose to die alone. On the other hand, others choose specifically to die in the company of their loved ones.

AFTER DEATH CARE
EXPERIENCES

In institutions and hospitals, the care for the deceased is called 'laying out'. Laying out is the preparing, washing, and dressing of the deceased, ready for viewing. It is performed after the doctor has confirmed death and always in accordance with the wishes of the deceased. This always used to be carried out by nursing staff and carers, but nowadays it's more common to see the last offices performed by funeral directors.

In hospices, we call this office the 'after death care'. In 'De Vier Vogels' Hospice, the Johannes Hospitium, and the Kajan Hospice, the hospice caregivers do it themselves, sometimes together with family members and friends, or by family under the supervision of a last offices group or a nurse. This is done in accordance with the wishes and possibilities of involved loved ones, for whom these can become precious memories in the future.

Nurse Mieke:

> My experience is that people often find it a little eerie, but if you invite them to be a part of it and guide them properly, they are often capable of doing the most beautiful things. They are then thankful that they have been able to help. For example, giving father a shave, putting mother's make-up on, or anything else to help during after death care.

The resident has discussed his or her wishes beforehand with one of the coordinators, usually together with their nearest and dearest. They will talk about what clothes they want to wear and other personal items such as jewellery, false teeth or glasses. Then they talk about who will carry out the last offices, who will keep vigil before, during, and after death and about the viewing period. It isn't always possible to agree on this beforehand. Sometimes death can occur so soon after admission that we don't have time to talk about the resident's final wishes.

Lisette:

> One gentleman had only been in the hospice for half a day. He had brought hardly any clothes and no personal belongings at all. He died that same evening. I looked around the hospice to find clothes for him but it didn't feel right for him to wear someone else's things. I managed to find something in his cupboard and so by following my instincts, I was able to care for him very well. His nephew was deeply touched by it.

When does life actually end and when is someone really dead? Is it the moment that the heart stops beating and blood stops pumping and the attending doctor has confirmed death? If that's the case, then how is it that hospice caregivers regularly feel a presence after the physical death? A 'something' that dissipates or slowly lets go, but can still be felt? Anthroposophy states that the three days that follow death are still a part of the biography of man. It is an 'interval' in which we care and surround the deceased so they will be able to look back at the lives they have led. It's a time in which the bodily life is freed through images. Peace and serenity are needed to view life's panorama, which unfolds for the dying like a film played backwards. From early times in Eastern traditions, but also in various movements within Western esoteric Christianity, much is known about the new life that the deceased enters.

'The world is more complex than the simple mechanical model we have followed for so long. The evidence suggests that we are more than brain function and that "something" – soul, spirit or consciousness – will continue in some form or another for a while at least', according to Peter and Elizabeth Fenwick on the back cover of their book *The Art of Dying.*

Annelies wonders about this question too:

> When does life stop and when is someone dead? When I'm sitting
> with someone who has died, I can still feel a presence for half an hour
> or an hour afterwards. A person might have died physically but I feel
> that the energy, the soul, is still there. I always wait until the soul has
> departed before I carry out the last offices. I am so glad that here in
> this hospice we are sometimes allowed to wait for hours for the soul
> to be at peace before we begin the care after death. In my experience,
> the families also want us to give the soul that time of peace.

Nurse Mieke:

> Recently, I was with a lady who always used to lie rigid and stiff in
> her bed, but who, after her death, became very supple, and had such
> a relaxed expression on her face. It was as though death had brought
> her the relaxation that she could never find while she was alive. She
> also 'looked' quite beatifically out of her eyes.

In hospices, perhaps more than in other places, you will find
rituals surrounding the care after death. There are sure to be differences in certain areas, but there are mainly many similarities.
When a resident dies, families and friends can find it meaningful
to light a special candle and then to blow it out when the deceased
leaves the hospice. Usually residents who have died stay for one
day before they are collected by the funeral directors. In the Kajan Hospice, they cover the deceased residents with a special quilt,
unless the family wishes otherwise. Workers who are in the hospice at the time generally attend the candle ritual and say farewell.
They share thoughts and memories about the resident's time at the
hospice, someone might read a poem, well wishes are spoken, there
will be a few moments of silence, whatever seems right for that person. Then the funeral director arrives and the deceased is placed
in the coffin and taken away. This is also done in accordance with
the wishes and facilities, together with family, friends and/or hospice caregivers. In the hall of De Vier Vogels, they sound the gong.
Those involved will follow the coffin outside and wait there until
the funeral car is out of sight.

The after death care takes place in a sheltered atmosphere, in the
sense that people won't be walking in and out. The last offices respect

both the deceased and death itself. Those who carry out the care after death often find themselves in an atmosphere that transcends normal daily consciousness. It's a kind of timelessness. When everything has been done, it is important that they take a moment for themselves, have something to eat and drink, and gradually get back to their daily routine. I can well remember the last offices I carried out for a lady who had been with us for some time. Although the traces of her illness were visible, you could still see the robust blonde lady she once was, and whose photos on the wall were living proof. Her partner visited her regularly. A huge, burly man with tattoos all over his arms, rings through his ears, and as soon as he was outside, a large roll-up between his lips. Her daughters, from different relationships, would come and go, full of emotion. On the afternoon she died, a colleague and I carried out the after death care. It was physically draining, but it was nothing compared to what we both experienced later that evening. It was as though we were covered by a blanket of lead. An oppressive, heavy, almost stifling weariness that could not just be the result of our physical efforts. We were threatened by the energy of this lady who not surprisingly, given her eventful and difficult life, was called 'The Gypsy Queen'.

An impressive and moving ritual at the close of the after death care is the oiling of the hands. Hands that have worked for an entire life. Hands that have cradled and carried, beaten and caressed, given and taken, held close and let go. These hands deserve a final honour, and then they can rest. It is a ritual that often evokes awe, respect, and gratitude for the life that person has lived.

Lisette:

> We had a lady who had two sons with whom she'd had a falling out. Her sister wanted to help with the after death care as a tribute, and she also called the two sons. The relationship with these sons had always been difficult. They were both addicted to alcohol and drugs. They came to say goodbye to their mother, but didn't want to stay with her. When it was over, I asked them if they wanted to be there for the oiling of hands. I asked them if they wanted to do it. It was so moving to see these big, rough men with hands like shovels thanking their mother for what her hands had done for them.

Lisette and Annelies, both members of the last offices and vigil group, talk about their experiences in the hours when after death care takes place and how it can feel as if someone is still there. Annelies:

When a resident dies I am called in. When I go into the room, sometimes there is a voice, or something that speaks to me: 'Wait. Leave me for a moment, leave me alone ...' and then I wait. Sometimes I think: 'I have to wait a bit longer.' Then I wait a while longer, hopefully if the family also wants me to. Then at one point I feel that it's allowed. I'm given permission, I can go ahead. And at that moment when I begin, when I feel that I've been given permission, then the care I provide for the deceased goes so well. I always call the residents by their Christian names, always. Do I sometimes begin too soon? Yes ... if the family say: 'We have been at the bedside for three nights. We want to go home, let's just start.' I can understand that they are exhausted, and so we begin. And then I encounter difficulties. I have to deal with a rigid body, with resistance. So, that permission, listening to that inner voice, is very important to me.

Lisette:

We had a resident who used to be a nurse. She had always been in control, and found it difficult to admit to being vulnerable, to have someone else in charge. She also didn't want any fuss made over her death. She didn't want her husband to come when she died, she wanted to be taken straight to the funeral parlour. I carried out the after death care and it was so strange, we couldn't close her eyes. I tried everything, but then her sister said: 'Just leave them open'. It was as though she wanted to supervise everything about her death. During the last offices I emptied her bladder as much as possible, but the next day – and this never happens – she was wet. Not just a bit, but she was wet through to her shroud, and we had to take care of her again. It was as though she could only really let go after she died.

Is it necessary to know someone in order to carry out the after death care properly? How can you connect to someone you hardly know, or don't even know at all? The following experiences told by Lisette show that it's possible to connect with the energy of the deceased in such a way, so that the care after death can still, or even for that reason, be carried out properly.

Lisette:

When I'm performing the after death care, I often have the feeling that someone is still there. By being still and taking the time to feel, or perhaps by playing some music, I can sense what the right thing to do will be. Then, for example, I can select a particular colour for the shroud, or use a particular object. I don't know why I do. It just seems right, even though I haven't known the person well. Afterwards we get the reaction: 'that is exactly what my mother or my father looked like. Now can I recognise them again.' Or: 'Oh, you've put that there', about a book that I've left open on a particular page. Or: 'Goodness, fancy choosing that one, it was always her favourite book.' I remember that of all the books we could have chosen for one gentleman, we decided on one about the war. It seems that he had struggled with that all his life. The family said: 'Now it's there with him, the struggle is over.' And then I was told the whole story by the family.

I remember a lady who I hadn't known well at all. The person in charge, who had known the lady longer, had chosen the clothes. I set out the clothes, but had the feeling that they weren't right for the woman who was lying there, even though I had never seen her fully dressed. I looked in her wardrobe and eventually found something that I thought would suit her better. I asked: 'Can I change this?' It was allowed, and then the person in charge came to look and said: 'Yes, that's exactly how she was!' How did I connect with this lady? I had found a copied CD and thought, this is the kind of music she liked. By listening to it, I got a better idea of who she was and was able to connect with her. I didn't do it to get compliments, but it was wonderful to hear that it was just like her and to know that I hadn't made her into a dress-up doll. This is the lady as she was. That pleases me. We were in tune, it was something I could do for her.

Another resident with whom I had almost no contact was due to have euthanasia at 4 o'clock one day. I was in my car and around that time I suddenly felt very hot and had the urge to watch the film *Departures*.[14] I'd had this film at home for some time, but had never found the time to watch it. I came home, sat down and watched the film, which I

---

[14] *Departures, the gift of last memories.* A film by Yojiro Takita, 2009, Wild Bunch.

found very moving. Later on I was called and asked to carry out the after death care. Because I had watched this movie I was so tuned in that, although scarcely knowing this resident, I was able to take very good care of him.

Lisette has many more examples of after death care, whereby it is so important to be attuned to the person: 'I often do that by staying quietly in the room, listening to their own music, and by talking to them. I am often prompted in the right direction. The family is always so moved when after the after death care has been done, they can once again see the person they have loved.'

Strictly speaking, after death care isn't covered by Fenwick's research, but it came up over and over again in the interviews. They are real and meaningful experiences. Not just for the loved ones, but because they show that the consciousness does not end when the body dies.

Death is not a single event, but a process. And so we discover that death is not an ending but a transition. Hospice caregivers are able to offer us profound insights into the state of consciousness and perceptions of the transition area surrounding death.

THE ROLE OF THE HOSPICE WORKER

In hospices, time and attention are amply available whereas in other institutions time and attention are quite often lacking. Because hospices are small-scale, they can provide each resident with personal attention, and no distinction is made between philosophies, religions, or backgrounds. Hospices want to provide a safe and dependable environment, where the dying can prepare for the end of their lives, and can grow accustomed to the idea of the approaching parting with loved ones. As well as the professional medical and nursing care, there are also the volunteers, who have time and attention to give from within their own experiences and personalities.

Volunteer Cok tells how she actually makes contact with a resident:

When I'm quiet and calm within, I can pick up on more things around me. It could be that the other person notices it and a connection is made. Yes, this really is what I experience. It's about making connection. I think you can take good care of someone, but that's not the same as making a connection. You can do what you're meant to do, leave the room knowing you have done your job, but that's different from making a connection. For example, there was a gentleman who was with us for a couple of days. He was still getting used to everything. He had come to us from a nursing home where he had received little care. I gave him thickened water because he had such difficulty swallowing. He was busy trying not to choke and I was busy trying not to let him choke. I took everything back to the kitchen, went back, straightened up a chair and went back to check on him once more to be sure. Moving closer to him and making eye contact, I asked him in a different way: 'Can I do anything for you, can I be of help in any way?' He frowned, he was quiet, thought about it then suddenly said, 'Yes, yes, pray for me.' If I hadn't made that real connection and had just done my job, I would have missed that. Then you miss it altogether. It is so important: every single time, take a deep breath before you go in.

Volunteer Tina spoke about how busy she had been in the past year. She said:

It seems when you are under pressure yourself that you're less receptive to these phenomena, these end-of-life experiences. I believe that very strongly. In a way, I was given proof of it. I had in fact been ill and thought: I'm doing absolutely nothing for a few days. After three days, I had this strong urge to call someone I hadn't seen for a long time, and who was very ill. It turned out that at that very moment, she had actually taken a turn for the worse. I honestly believe that this impulse came to me because I had been so calm inside after three days of rest. You need to keep your ear to the ground but, when you're busy and under pressure, you can't do that. For me, this has been a real insight in the past year. I try to keep my own daily pressures outside. In any case, being with a person who is dying helps you to get to another awareness level.

In order to respond properly to the needs of the dying, rest and just slowing things down are essential. In this respect, hospice volunteers learn the so-called 'threshold exercise', which allows them to become conscious of what they could take with them into the dying person's room: their own turmoil, everyday worries, or thoughts about all the things they have to do. Everything from the shopping list to taking care of the neighbours' cats while they are on holiday, or preparing for a meeting or for the birthday party that evening, not to mention one's own expectations, insecurities, assumptions and beliefs. The threshold exercise allows you to leave all your own concerns behind, to go in with an open mind, to be receptive and to make non-judgemental observations. When the threshold exercise isn't done, it can damage the atmosphere in the room. Lisette had such an experience when her father was staying in the hospice. It made her more aware of her own role.

Lisette:

> End-of-life experiences and the way in which I make a connection with some residents, challenges me to be more receptive, to be more sensitive. What does the resident want to tell me by making a certain gesture or giving a particular glance and how can I respond with even fewer words or gestures? I myself noticed when my own father was in the hospice how a particular atmosphere in a room can be shattered by someone coming into the room and making a comment such as: 'We're having green beans for dinner this evening'. I notice that it is so important to take the time to just be, to just feel. I think that others need this too. I have learned to enter a room quietly and fully aware and, if I'm not needed, to leave again. I actually need to create a bond on a non-verbal level. Yes, my role seems to be to feel and tune into what is needed on a non-verbal level. I keep my antennae sharpened so that I need fewer and fewer words, because it's on that level that only what needs to be said is said, and I don't want to go charging in like a bull in a china shop.

Hospice supervisor Simone talks about this kind of atmosphere:

> It's obvious to me that there are greater forces present that surround the dying process and that something happens within that energy which is mind-expanding. It is a fragile and very special period for the person who is dying and those who are close. A glimpse of something greater.

In every single interview with the hospice caregivers, I was able to discern a specific role. A role influenced by a special talent that was not necessarily linked to the position of that individual. Everyone is born with a particular gift, a unique talent that you use as a natural resource, something that you can't help using and which makes you feel free, energized and inspired. We can't learn that talent, it is something we bring with us and can develop. Even if we haven't yet fully developed our unique talent, it doesn't detract from our unique individuality. It is this that is demonstrated when hospice caregivers seem to rise above the everyday consciousness. It is a moment when they are totally subservient to the dying process.

Simone, supervisor, tells us that she was so focused on the theme end-of-life experiences during her research year, that it consumed her thoughts and she felt the threat of no longer being receptive to it.

Simone:

> Yes, but not just because of the study, also because of the ongoing daily administrative work. That also calls for mind work. It's not the best way to remain tuned in to the needs of the residents. With a study like this I also think: maybe I will experience something, but that doesn't help me. It requires an openness and letting go of all preconceived ideas. You get into a kind of flow where things fall into place and can happen. The research made me more aware. It has nothing to do with reasoning. Well, maybe it does when you look back, but not in that moment. Yes, that's something too, being in the moment with all your senses. It isn't focussed concentration, more an open state of consciousness. It is intensity. That's helpful for me and for everything surrounding the dying process. My role is mainly to oversee and stay attuned with what's happening. Like with the lady: 'Can your friend just come and say hello?' I didn't even think about it, it just happened. Yes, that was because I was tuned in to what was going on around me.

Supervisor Suzanne talks about the need for subtlety when dealing with the end-of-life experiences of the dying. Especially when it comes to the family.

Suzanne:

> It's as though I drop a tealeaf into a cup and wait to see if it reaches the bottom. If it doesn't, then I'll stop doing it. So if, for example, I talk to one of the sisters alone, she might have received the tealeaf but because her brothers are there, she doesn't dare to talk about it. That is clearly my role, to look for atonement as subtly as a swirling tealeaf. For instance, if their mother experiences something, then I will indicate that maybe she's getting a signal from 'above'. This gives them reassurance. It's important to reassure the family, because everything around the deathbed can be frightening. They feel helpless, their mother didn't want this. It is therefore always difficult for the family. It's easier for me. Of course sometimes I'm

powerless too, but I still try to create a kind of foundation. And I always fit in there somewhere myself, sometimes more profound than other times.

The process of dying is a process that belongs solely to the dying person and the question is whether or not carers are able to respect this process. It requires not only an expanded awareness of the mind, but also insight into what death actually is in order to leave the process to the dying and not to take over or connect exclusively to the job or task at hand. Mieke, who has worked in terminal care for fifteen years, knows how to maintain a balance. Mieke's role, beyond her job as a nurse, is mainly 'doing by not doing', wu wei as it is called in Taoism.

Mieke:

> I always try to let people do things for themselves, what they are able to do, what they want to do and what they can cope with. Without controlling or managing. But I do try to stay close to them. Of course, sometimes I have to take over or do something in my professional capacity, but I try to just be there as a person. Yes, I let the person deal with the process. We had a resident who had drifted far away, but I still used to sit with him. Not because I just wanted to but because I felt that there was some reason why I should stay. I knew I was doing something by not doing anything. Sometimes I will talk or try to involve the family. Sometimes people don't know what to do or start to panic and I will try to guide them. For example I will say: 'Tell him that you love him, or that everything is fine.' In this way they can offer positive reassurance during that final stage rather than just only passing on their own grief. Not long ago there was a daughter who told me that she was so glad she'd done that. So it isn't just about what the dying themselves can do, but also what the family can contribute.

For some people, the role that calls for their intuitive talents is not always obvious. Usually because it just seems so logical to them. As volunteer Loes says: 'Hmm, yes ... what is my role? Yes, "I'm here", that's my role. I do believe that but don't really think about it.'

One experience described by Loes illustrates that she is there when and where she is really needed:

> I was with someone who died at that moment. His wife was terribly nervous. Her husband lay in bed and she kept asking: 'Is he going to die now, is he going to die now?' Then I replied: 'Yes ... I think so.' I could feel a certain atmosphere in the room. I was called away and needed to leave the room, but I didn't. I just stayed there. I somehow knew I had to stay there. When the lady started to panic so much about her husband dying, I held both of them tight. You could say I was a kind of link between them and, while holding them he breathed his last. It was so very special. The lady was very calm when her husband died. She asked: 'Is he dead now?' And I replied: 'Yes, he has died.' She stayed calm, and it was a strange and wonderful moment. It happened, and I was there. It was the most moving experience I have ever had, as it was for her.

Loes connected inwardly with her role and followed her instinct: I'm here. She didn't leave the room even though she had been called away, even though she wasn't sure that the gentleman was about to die.

Volunteer Tina:

> I don't think that I have a role. I just let it happen. It is just the way it is. I am there but I don't try to have a role.

The uniqueness which is expressed by hospice caregivers is something beyond the personal. It goes beyond thought, beyond judgement. However illustrative these examples might be, it is often hard to put into words what this uniqueness entails. Earlier we heard from Jeannie, who kept her eyes focussed on a resident who was dying.

She [Jeannie] says:

> Being there. Just that ... that's what springs to mind now. Just being there. I was there when the lady made her transition.

Joke says:

> How would I describe my role? Yes ... presence. This role unfolds itself so that I can tune in. It's a matter of being there and making space

for the other's needs. That's what I've learned, that's what I want too. Sometimes I feel myself being sucked in and then I have to be alert to keep my own space. Then I can't be my natural self anymore because I go along with the other person and let my head rule too much. It keeps me from giving the best attention and being there for the people.

Cynthia, volunteer:

If I think about my presence at the bedside, I would describe my role as a 'sounding board'. People want to get things off their chest and just want someone to listen. And I'm there for them. So just listening without saying anything, just taking it in. What I will often do is touch someone. I'm a very tactile person. I hold my hand out and they will usually put their hand in mine. But now we're talking about it, I wonder if it's really necessary. I have a feeling I should do as little as possible. Certainly not say anything, just stay reserved.

Jos, volunteer:

I am a listener. I've noticed that when I try something, it backfires. I work better when I just listen. And it's easier for me because I don't have to worry if I've said the right thing or not. Yes, I have the inner capacity to be a listener.

Sometimes it is awkward to apply that naturally-felt talent, because there are uncertainties in what one's place should be. This was the case with a volunteer who tells how it can sometimes be a dilemma for her when a nurse is focused on her task, and she seems to see the bigger picture.

I'm a volunteer. The nurse takes care of the patient and I help her. I see a lot, I do a lot and I know a lot, but I don't say much because I have a feeling that the nursing staff know the same things. Yes, I am discreet but sometimes I find it hard to take a back seat. I don't want to push myself forward and take over but I sense and I know so much. Yes, I am someone who knows and I find it difficult sometimes, which leaves me insecure. Because, yes, I'm here for a reason.

Some hospice caregivers consciously tap into the connection with their inner talents.

Ruth:

Here in the hospice, we once had a talents workshop, and everyone was extremely shy. It was emphasised that only you could name your own talent. So everyone would say something like, 'You are so good at taking care of people'. But no, those are qualities. If someone else says you have a good attribute, then that is a quality. That's a bonus. You can only identify your talent yourself. You could look back in your past: what interested me as a child, what is the common thread in my life, what did I want to learn? Then I came up with the word 'friendship'. I want to just be there for people. Friendship in a kind of unquestioning way. Nourished, because I consciously feel and recognise that feeling because my name is Ruth. Ruth means 'female friend'. Therefore, I am honouring my name.

One morning a couple of years later, I woke up and, as I woke up, I had to cry. I thought I was being told that I should intensify that word 'friendship' into 'guardianship'. Meanwhile, my course in life meant that I was present at a lot of births, and I was also with many people who were dying. So I heard that I had to intensify that friendship into guardianship. That's really what I want to do. Carefully and modestly at that gateway, as a witness to both the coming and the going. Yes, 'being born' has actually become the theme of my life.

Hilly:

How would I describe or call my role? Yes, there is a term used by more people in another context, but it's a word that I connect to very strongly: midwifery. In the same way you might see the role of a midwife at a birth, that's how I see my role with the dying. There are also many things that happen that I don't have a clear picture of. Even so, I've always felt that I am seeing the larger context. Now and then I don't see it, but I still feel that everything is as it should be. Yes, it calls for trust. That trust has grown in the last few years. When I had just got back from my Music Thanatology studies in America, I still felt very uncertain in this field. I've come to see that, in my role with the harp, I can move through the whole spectrum. On the one side it can be seen as entertainment, but way over on the other side it is a state of consciousness. I have learned to move within that spectrum and I try to be very careful with my interpretations. But yes, when I think of my role, I have a very clear image of a midwife.

Willy:

> My job is that of a nurse but my biggest job to myself is to give everyone space. It's who I am. I'm a Libra, which means I am also indecisive and hesitant. I see one side of the coin, followed immediately afterwards by the other side. This can make it hard to make a proper decision, but the positive side is that I can tell when someone is telling the truth, or if that person is only telling me part of the truth. I don't have any difficulty in not judging people. It's often the more eccentric people who are my favourites because they are vulnerable and a bit crazy. I also like people with psychiatric illnesses, while others often find them harder to deal with. Yes, I think that's because of the inner space I possess. I always try to make a connection so that the other can have the space to really be him or herself.

Volunteer Anke is very sure about her role:

> A fellow human being. It's a deep need within to be there for someone, whoever it might be. Yes, without any prejudgement or favouritism. It doesn't matter who or what they are. There is only this moment.

When hospice caregivers in their care for the dying go beyond thinking and perceive without making judgements, they will be able to ask: what is needed here? Then they can tend to the dying intuitively, relate to what is happening, and do what is necessary.

Cocky, with more than twenty years' experience in palliative nursing care, talks about her role:

> I look at what the dying and those around them really need. Should I stay or not, and if I should stay, why? So, I observe very carefully. And this applies both to the dying and to the family. So, I look at what needs to be done and respond as best I can. Sometimes I only see it afterwards. Sometimes people will rally one last time. I had a comatose patient who suddenly wanted something to eat. He died the next day. A revival like that is a sign that it can happen soon, but you only realise afterwards. Even so, I know intuitively what needs

to be done. This isn't about procedures but about feelings. You have
to be open and sensitive.

Caring for the dying out of need for acknowledgment, recognition
or reward is a care that is born from poverty. It isn't implausible for
the carers or loved ones to take control of the situation in an attempt
to satisfy their own unfulfilled needs. Unconsciously, the other person is used for the carer's own needs. If we know our own needs and
rise above them, then we can offer service from a position of wealth.
That requires a profound inner balance between giving and receiving.
When giving and receiving are in perfect balance and feelings become
awareness, service arises from abundance. Feelings become awareness
and no longer have anything to do with those involved as personalities,
but rather with seeing things as they really are. Awareness assumes
a pure consciousness and hospice caregivers become merely tools so
that everyone and everything around the deathbed is able to become
a meaningful whole. This development path in service is dynamic and
many hospice caregivers with whom I have spoken are aware of it.

WHAT THESE EXPERIENCES CAN MEAN TO THE DYING AS WELL AS TO FAMILY, FRIENDS AND HOSPICE CAREGIVERS

———————⟫●⟨———————

Those who have never dealt with end-of-life experiences as described in this book, can quite easily dismiss them as fantasy or as some kind of disorientation or confusion. However, once people have gone through such an event themselves, it leaves behind a deep and lasting impression. It's not unusual for such people to see death in an entirely different light. Many gain new insights into what death actually is and find deep meaning in both life and death. For the dying themselves, end-of-life experiences generally seem to offer comfort, encouragement and reassurance.

As one of the hospice caregivers told us:

> Residents quite often tell us that they have seen and met people who have died, and how wonderful that was. That it made them feel happy and they wanted to talk about it. This shows me that it brings comfort.

These end-of-life experiences also seem to prepare the dying for death and take away their fear of death.

Anke, volunteer:

> It also takes away the fear of dying. Not what happens before, but knowing that once it's time then all will be well. Then it will be safe, someone will be waiting. Yes, this kind of experiences definitely diminishes fear.

For many relatives, a sense of reassurance also arises from these experiences, unless fear prevails. In that case they will dismiss them as nonsense, consider them laughable, or not notice them at all. It may also be that relatives don't talk about them because it's unfamiliar and seems unreal. It's just easier not to mention them.

Suzanne, supervisor:

> I have noticed that the dying always accept what happens. The family are not always as convinced. Then they say something like: 'It's because of the medicine or she's hallucinating.' I find that end-of-life experiences are often dismissed as non-existent, especially when the family is together. They don't want to go any deeper, half of them keep their distance.

Nurse Willy:

> Some people laugh about it, others are able to handle it well. Some are unsure: exactly what is happening here? It's at these moments when guiding becomes first priority. I always ask the family: 'Would you like me to come in every half an hour, or would you rather just do this together?' They still like it when I go in now and again, and I can keep explaining what is happening.

Volunteer Anke is not so sure how the relatives feel about it:

> I find that difficult. No, I'm not sure how comforting these end-of-life experiences are for the families. What's comforting is that a loved one becomes more calm. But I am not sure what it does to a family when the dying person tells them about such an experience. I also don't

know if a dying person talks about it. But if the person who is dying can pass on in peace, it offers comfort for them.

Volunteer Helen found solace in the religiously tinted end-of-life experiences of her father and can imagine that it also brings comfort to the families of those dying in the hospice:

> Yes, it helped us a great deal. It meant I could carry on. I definitely see it as a consolation. I also find it hard when someone doesn't have something to hold on to. When people suffer a great deal of sadness or pain, I always ask: 'can you hold on to your faith?' Some people can and that makes me happy. I can identify with them because I'm a religious person myself. It makes me sad when people don't have faith to hold on to. Sometimes I will ask: 'Would you like me to pray for you' or I will say: 'I am praying for you.' But of course, I cannot force my religious beliefs on others.

Hospice caregivers recognise and describe end-of-life experiences as meaningful, valuable and real. They enrich them and humble them at the same time, as Anita explained earlier:

> I feel even more humble now. We can only do so much. We do a wonderful job, but you mustn't overestimate yourself or try to make yourself important or try to do more than you are capable of. Yes, it humbles you. How does it make me feel when people share their dreams with me? I find it wonderful because it allows me to get close to someone and feel the essence of life. It is fragile, tangible and very real. The true meaning of what it is to be human.

Anke:

> It always makes me silent. I feel silent when I receive these things and makes me silent to be able to experience them. To have the trust of people who want to share the experiences with me, it changes me. I think it makes me even more sensitive. It's a confirmation that I did the right thing. I felt something, I did something, and it was right. It gives me inner security. It gives me confidence that I can trust in myself.

Some hospice caregivers change a great deal by being present at a deathbed, and others gain deep inner knowledge. Sometimes they lose

their fear of death altogether, which is an ideal situation when you are by the side of someone who is dying.

Annelies:

> These experiences have definitely changed me. I'm a very down to earth, medically trained woman, with over 35 years of experience in a hospital run by managers for whom only one word counts, 'efficiency'. I tried to show that there was another way but was not taken seriously. I slowly made a move away from the strict healthcare regime with its protocols to a wider world. I found that here it exists as it should. I have become another person. I look at death completely differently. I was always very afraid and a great supporter of euthanasia. Absolutely, if anyone was for euthanasia, it was me. But now that I'm here, in the hospice, I actually think: how could I have thought that? I turned the full 180 degrees. Now I try to shed light on the other side, also towards others: this too is life, dying is part of it, these moments are so precious.

Simone, supervisor:

> These experiences change me, absolutely. As well as being incredibly moving, I can also really feel the connection and I am so conscious of it, especially afterwards. I long to be connected like that every minute, to continually practice it to be in the here and now. Then I feel as though I am in a stream that is totally healing for me and for others. It's a continual exercise. I also feel that I am being helped in this and that I am connected to everyone, and then it just happens, things unfold.

Hilly, music therapist:

It fits in with who I am and at the same time it changes me as a person. The most remarkable thing is that I really have no fear of death. I can be afraid of suffering, but I am not afraid of dying and can cope with it very well. The expression 'dead easy' is really fitting. It has changed me, and most people think that I made this career change at an illogical moment. I was a radiologist, but then I went to America to study Music-Thanatology, a huge change in my life. When I look back, it was primarily the vision of that friend who was able to find me in Italy and the experiences at my mother's deathbed which determined the enormous switch I made, on top of my experiences as a child.

Volunteer Tini:

I find it quite natural, it hasn't changed me. I feel very happy when it happens, because I get the impression that it's very comforting for the person dying. I think that relatives also find it beautiful and comforting. It's the last thing someone does or says and it touches us in a different way. Yes, because they still experience it together.

Nurse Mieke:

It doesn't change me. It's quite normal really. I also have the sensation sometimes that someone is sitting on my bed. It's good that deceased loved ones are around me. I don't see it, it's just an experience. When residents share something with me, I don't think that they are sharing it with me specifically. They are just people who can share it and would share it with another person too. It's nice to think they can share it with me though.

Suzanne, supervisor:

These experiences give me goose bumps. To know that there is room for this, here in the hospice, motivates me to do this job. I find it a comforting thought that there is something beautiful on the other side. I see a smile on the faces of almost everyone who has died. Not with everyone, but I often see that someone's suffering is over and that all is well on the other side. For me they are 'aha' experiences. I think that I was born that way, that I already knew it, and now I can say it out loud. So, it's a kind of recognition as well as a motivation to do this work.

Wilma, nurse:

I keep growing as a person. The fact that I can experience this special moment, that's truly enriching. Some people think: oh, death is so awful. But we live here, we applaud life. If you could see what goes on here. There is a lot of laughter, it's so pure. Nobody here hides behind a façade. When you can be with people in all their tenderness, their awakening, without any fuss, without frills! That is enriching, it's just lovely!

DEALING
WITH DEATH

Unlike hospice caregivers, for most people death is a taboo subject. They push away all thoughts about the end of life and avoid talking about it. In our current Western culture we aren't used to dealing with death and the journey towards it. Up to the mid-twentieth century, most people used to die at home, with their families around them and in their own community. Death was an accepted part of life. Much has changed since then. Thanks to medical advances, we live longer and most of us now die in a hospital or an institution. Dying has therefore become a medicalised process and we are less and a less part of it. The sad truth is that many of us have never been near someone when they are at the point of death. The result is fear and many are even horrified at the thought of a dead body. Our collective fear leaves us unprepared when someone near to us becomes terminally ill and will die. We don't know what to expect, how to react, and how to support our loved ones. This is especially true in hospitals where the focus lies on getting better and treatment is the dominant decision maker.

Christine Longaker argues that the dying want us to relate to them as living, compassionate people and to accept their vulnerability and suffering, and at the same time see them as whole. But how can we be there for them when our hearts remain closed through fear, when sickness, old age and dying don't fit in with our successful and controllable lives, when we are unknowing and unprepared to surrender our own vulnerability? Knowing what to expect can help us to examine our own fears and to make a loving, supportive contribution to this valuable and essential process.

THE PROCESS
OF DYING

Every person dies in their own way. That is not the same thing as saying that people will die as they have lived. Their own, unique way of dying does of course say something about how someone has lived, but that cliché leaves no room for the growth and change that occurs on the deathbed. And it is in dying that we can see people move towards softening and vulnerability. The process of dying can be slow, but it can also happen within a few hours. Just as we are formed in the womb from the four elements of earth, water, fire and air, so the four elements leave us one by one as we are dying. The element ether plays a specific role.[15]

First, the earth element leaves us, resulting in loss of weight, physical strength and matter. Energy declines. Then the element of water disappears and the body dehydrates. There is then a loss of control of the bodily fluids, causing incontinence, excessive sweating, a runny nose and ear discharge. The element of fire is the next to leave us. People feel cold. It starts in the body's extremities: the hands, feet, ears and nose. The organs begin to dry out and the warmth retreats towards the heart. Finally, the element of air will go. Breathing becomes shallower; there

---

[15] From: Marinus Hummelen (2000). *Bewust sterven, handboek voor sterven en stervensbegeleiding.(Dying consciously: guide for dying and hospice care)* Utrecht: Servire/Kosmos-Z&K Uitgevers B.V.

can be shortness of breath until it eventually stops altogether. It's such a powerful and impressive experience to witness how the bodily matter is actually broken down: the detachment from the earth. Then there are the more subtle energies that dissolve, less visible to the untrained senses, but experiences you can read about in this book, which bring stillness. When we look at the dissolution of the elements from a larger perspective, then the element of earth represents the parting from the earth, from all our possessions, from all material things. When the water element dissolves, we are taking leave of all our emotions. The element of fire stands for the soul that is leaving the earth, and finally with the element of air, we breathe out our last breath and we pass over to the spiritual world, or the world of the soul.

Specific indications can make us aware that illness or old age turn into preparation for death. For example, people will withdraw from the outside world and their own world will become smaller and smaller. Occasionally residents will go home for a visit outside the hospice and sometimes they will sit in the conservatory or garden, but then they will become more withdrawn and stay in their own rooms, where family and friends can visit. As time goes on, they will have fewer visitors, until just their circle of close friends and family remain. Eventually, the dying person will no longer want to get out of bed.

> She was able to say goodbye to her own home one last time. Then she took to her bed. Did she know she was going to die? She never left her bed again. She was tired and could feel her strength ebbing away.

The dying are usually well aware as the time approaches, but sometimes the signs are not always clear or they are misunderstood.

Tina tells us:

> We had a lady, a little simple, with an intellectually challenged brother, her husband and her sister-in-law. They would visit every day and she liked that. Then one day she told them: 'You don't need to come tomorrow.' She was perfectly lucid and alert so we thought, it will be a while yet. The cleaning lady who looked after her room had said: 'See you tomorrow.' The lady looked at her and shook her head. She died the next day. She had felt it so clearly, and yes, we here in the hospice hadn't felt anything at all. It wasn't feeling, it was knowing, it was so clear, no confusion.

Needing more sleep can be a sign that the body is preparing itself for death, with a footnote that extreme exhaustion is one of the most important symptoms for cancer patients. However, when long periods of sleep alternate with lucid and wakeful moments, it can be a sign. Apart from the physical process, dying is also an internal process which is exhausting and can demand a lot from a patient. As the end approaches, we see an increase in the transit from one reality to another.

Tini talks about one resident:

> This gentleman was very cynical. He said: 'Keep everyone away, they don't need to come because I'm dying anyway.' His daughter still managed to visit him however. At one point he was so far away, but then he came back. He had been somewhere where he had felt so comfortable, where he was content. Slowly but surely his cynicism began to disappear. He was calmer, but still kept travelling back and forth. Then he said: 'I thought I was already there.' It was nice to know that he had become less cynical, because he died the next day.

When death is in sight, the body knows that it no longer needs sustenance, and the dying will lose their appetite for food and drink. A natural thing. That is the earth element leaving the body. Some just accept this, others will try to eat for as long as possible. Sometimes it seems to be an attempt to delay death, but it is more often likely to be the habit of a lifetime of eating and an almost instinctive attempt to cling on to life. I remember a gentleman who was used to eating dinner at 6 o'clock every evening, and who was so surprised to find that he had lost his appetite.

Nurse Cocky:

> There was a lady who had been coping well for a long time, but who became upset and confused when she had to let others do things for her. It was so difficult for her. Eventually, she was confined to bed. She lay in bed, still lucid, and asked if she could have something to eat. You could see that her hands were blue, her legs covered in spots, she felt cold, and clammy and was short of breath. However, she was still looking around quite brightly and couldn't accept what was happening. We gave her a massage, and an hour later she died. She had actually been dying but just couldn't accept it. We could see that

she had died, but her spirit was still there. Her body just gave up. We thought it was so typical of her.

Special requests by the dying can also be an indication that they are preparing to die, such as visiting a special place, or listening to a certain piece of music, gathering family photos around them or wanting a last encounter with someone very special to them.

Ina, volunteer:

One of our residents, an 80-year-old lady, had been dying for several days. Her husband just sat by her bedside and kept talking about his young wife. That was so lovely. Wonderful. They had five children and they all adored their mother. Very loving. Father didn't leave her side for a moment. At one point he called for me and I went into the room. He was in a panic: 'She wants to sit up, she wants to sit up!' He held her tight so that she wouldn't fall over. I adjusted her bed to a lower setting because she wanted to write something and I thought: this is really important. She wanted to write a letter to her granddaughter because she thought she had some unfinished business with her. She kept on saying so. That's just what she did, and he sat next to her, holding her so she wouldn't fall. She wrote what she felt she had to write and then settled down again. I believe she died the next day.

Sometimes the dying will express their gratitude to their carers and relatives in preparation for their coming departure. Language may also change. When the dying start talking about: 'leaving', 'flying', 'going home', 'being taken home', 'going on a journey' or 'a doorway', then we should be open and alert.

Suzanne:

A volunteer and a nurse were looking after one of our ladies. She was losing consciousness, and suddenly mumbled 'open', and again 'open'. The nurse asked her: 'What is open?' After a while, she said very clearly: 'The doorway is open.' I don't know how long it was before she died. She had been floating between heaven and earth for a while.

Elisabeth Kübler-Ross also draws attention to the symbolic language used by the dying in her publications about dying and bereavement

counselling. She observes that many of the dying bring up the subject of their own deaths and the time of their deaths, albeit cloaked in images. For example, she writes about an old man who wanted to give her his walking stick. At first, she didn't take it seriously. It was only after he died a short time later that she realised what he was really trying to say when he made his offer. He couldn't actually walk without his stick. The fact that he wanted to give it away was a sign that he didn't need it any more. Later on she regretted that she hadn't had the presence of mind to sit down with him and talk about what was on his mind. Supervisor, Suzanne, told earlier in this book about the lady who clearly felt that her death was approaching, and asked her brother to take her coat and then her favourite cardigan home.

Supervisor Simone also had a similar experience:

> What really made an impression on me was a resident who had taken off jewellery, her watch, and her bracelets. She still wanted a drink. She said: 'I'm so thirsty, I'm as dry as a bone, I could drink a gallon of water'. Then you're busy doing this and that for someone who also wants to take off all her jewellery. Right then I thought: gee, it could be that this lady is going to die soon. It just flashed through my mind. She did indeed die the very next morning. It's as though you make a note for yourself, that you think: Goodness, could it be, because why should someone suddenly ...?

Ruth, nurse complementary care:

> When we were changing shifts, a carer told me about a lady who was talking about a doorway. This appealed to me because I am interested in the doorways of birth and of death. In my experience, you really do have to pass through something. But I didn't follow it up. Later I was with her and she was very ill indeed. I had the impression that she knew I was there, so I gave her a rhythmic massage.[16] Suddenly a song popped into my mind, a very old song: 'I see a door that is wide open, light is streaming through, it's a door I can walk through safely and there I will find peace.' I sang it to her very softly and it was a

---

[16] Rhythmic massage is a rhythmic touching of the skin, getting in touch with the finer perceptive processes, which in turn allows sensitive communication with the deeper organs and tissues. Essential oils, herbs and ointments are used. Source: MatriCaria, supplementary nursing care.

very intimate moment. The next day I heard that she had died and it was a beautiful moment. It's wonderful to know that you have shared such an intimate moment with someone. It's not something I plan, it just happens and I want to practice it more. It helps me if I meditate beforehand.

Sudden changes in the process, transpersonal and final meaning end-of-life experiences and an alteration in language are all indications that death is approaching, possibly within days or weeks.

Simone tells us that it helps her in her work as a supervisor to see where someone is in the process:

I always go on the alert when someone throws off their blankets. Then the trick is not to just sit there thinking but to find out what they need. I make sure that the atmosphere in the hospice is more attuned. When someone is dying in the hospice, there is a different atmosphere, a different energy. More serene. I watch over it carefully, to give the dying the space they need.

There are also smaller changes which call for alertness and attentiveness.

Volunteer Cynthia:

I have noticed that there is a period when people do want to be touched, they love to be given a massage. However, there comes a time when they no longer want that physical contact. Then they seem to be closer to death. Or they will push everything away, and only want a cold drink or some ice cream. To me, these are signs that the end is approaching, that they are on their way, that they are really on their way.

Learning to recognise the changes in language and behaviour allows us to be open to the needs of the dying and to be close to them in the hour of their death.

PHYSICAL ASPECTS
OF DEATH

It seems to be impossible to determine when death actually occurs. People can hover on the threshold between life and death for quite some time. It is easy to miss the final moment. Yet there are some physical indications that can be distinguished.

Congestion in the lungs can cause the breathing to become difficult, heavy and gurgling. Although this can be distressing for those nearby, it is perfectly normal and is caused by the build up of fluid and discharge in the throat. Yawning is another natural response even for those who are unconscious. Yawning causes more oxygen to be taken into the lungs.

Because of decreased fluid intake, the kidneys can lose their function and the urine will be the colour of tea. It can have a pungent odour. If the muscles in the body lose their function, it also reduces control of the bladder and sphincter muscles. This means that a catheter might have to be used. The body loses heat as the blood circulation slows down and hands, arms, feet and legs become pale and cold. Because the entire physical system is functioning less effectively, there is a build-up of blood, resulting in dark purple spots on the lower part of the back and on the legs. The changing metabolism of someone who is dying can create a penetrating smell of acetone. This can be very unpleasant. One way to improve the fragrance in the room is to burn lamps filled with essential oils. An old-fashioned remedy is to place saucers containing ground coffee around the room. Coffee has the ability to absorb odours.

Gineke, volunteer:

> One lady had constant diarrhoea, which to me was a sign that she was letting everything go. I wasn't at all surprised when she died the next morning.

Inner turmoil and agitation can sometimes cause restlessness and the person dying might even cry out. The nursing staff can provide medication. It can be difficult for the relatives.

Earlier, nurse Willy told us about explaining what is happening:

> It can be reassuring when there is someone nearby who knows what is happening, and can explain it. This is extremely important because otherwise people will just keep on asking for medication. One relative said: 'Oh, this is awful, we can't let this go on'. I can then explain that it is a necessary part of the dying process. Of course we try to alleviate it, but it remains an intrinsic part.

Gineke, volunteer:

> There was a man who constantly cursed and swore. He was so angry. I have to confess that I was a bit tired of him, and asked him. 'Why do you swear so much when you know we take such good care of you?' 'Yes I know, but you have no idea how much pain I'm in. Then he vomited, and there was an enormous clot of blood. He died quietly that night. He had rid himself of everything. First verbally, then physically. This can also be an important sign.

At one point, the dying will no longer respond. They can no longer speak and their breath rattles in the throat when the mouth is open. It sounds like snoring and can be quite disturbing to hear. When they have to breathe through the mouth, it becomes very dry. To alleviate this, softly dabbing with a damp gauze bandage or a special cotton bud tends to help.

Lisette, volunteer:

I was looking after him together with the nurse when I noticed that his nose was running and he was dribbling. I motioned with my eyes: look what's happening. We carried on very quietly. He could no longer communicate. He was lying on his side with his head in my arms and I said: 'I think he's gone.' We carefully completed the care. His stool was completely black.. This is something that happens a lot, this letting everything go. It also has a distinct smell. When someone is about to die I have often noticed a particular smell coming out of their mouth. I have often asked other volunteers, 'Can you smell that?' For me, it means that the end is near. I have noticed that smell especially with people who are taking a long time to die, who are very thin yet still holding on. It's an unpleasant smell and stays in your nostrils.

Sometimes you will see people in a curious, curled-up position like a baby, almost foetal.

The complementary care Nurse talks about it:

Bit by bit, I have come to see the similarities between the end of life and the beginning. Both depend on the surroundings, vulnerability, not yet being independent or having lost one's independence. I see a sort of reversal between being born and dying. The prostrate position that both find themselves in; the incontinence, the having to be supported and helped. All things that are difficult but also very natural.

Finally there will be a change in the breathing pattern. A loud, rattling breath alternates with quiet, peaceful breathing. As the end really approaches, the dying will only take occasional breaths. After one breath, nothing will happen for a few seconds, then there will be another breath. This is known as Cheyne-Stokes respiration.

Ruth talks about the death of her father:

It was a moving experience to see my father with Cheyne-Stokes respiration, which is very similar to contractions. We watched him struggle and detach from his body. My father was 92 years old. I had spoken to him the previous Sunday. He still loved life so much and wanted to stay forever. But then he began to deteriorate and I told him: 'but you can go, you know.' That was so difficult for me but I'm glad I said it. I visited him on the Tuesday. He was walking around his house and the carer who was there said: 'Shhh ...' We saw him walk all over the house, keeping close to the walls because he could hardly stand. Very quietly, he went into the kitchen where the Bible lay open. Then he went to lie on the bed, and began the Cheyne-Stokes respiration. Just like real contractions. Having contractions to be reborn somewhere else. The unrest, that's as functional as contractions are functional, because the gate is opened. As observers, we might see it as painful and difficult, but it's a pity to mute it by using medication. We can see them through it though. Initially allowing nature to take its course but, when it gets too much, then you can help, that's why you are a midwife or a loss expert. I am not against medication in itself.

Dying is the last task in life and it is a unique process. Not everyone will experience the physical aspects described above, but it is good to be aware of what might happen. For relatives, or for those who have not experienced a death before, it can be disquieting and fearful. People often say that their father or mother 'would not have wanted this'. But if you really think about it, who is the one who wouldn't want it? Isn't this more often about ourselves than about the dying? Is it not our own ignorance and lack of preparation? Is it not our own impotence and inability to endure it? Everyone experiences the dying process in his or her own unique way. There is no wrong or right way. To realise this allows us to stop judging what should or could be appropriate. This brings us to the question: What is needed here? Instead of: What do I need? We can open our hearts and just follow the stream, have the faith to respect the autonomous dying process as it unfolds. It helps to see things from the wider perspective of the elements, which disappear one by one.

And then the dying release their last breath. Even if we are prepared, it can still overwhelm us. Sometimes the dying will take some last jerking breaths when the heart and lungs stop working. Others will give one long breath, followed a few seconds later by what seems like another breath. This can be repeated a few times, which, if you are not prepared, can be very disturbing. It is actually the lungs expelling the last of the air.

Anita, volunteer, talks about her experience with the last breath:

This happened with a gentleman who came to us one afternoon, and I was on duty that evening. His condition seemed to be deteriorating, but it didn't look as though he was going to die. He was very quiet and wasn't in pain. I saw very well how a person is at first very alive and how the breathing becomes quieter and quieter. Initially I kept a very close eye on him, then I heard a voice in my head which said: 'Just go and sit on your own chair.' So I pushed my chair back and sat quietly, breathing with him. First of all, he was breathing so quickly that I could barely keep up with him. Then very gradually, it became calmer and slower. Eventually it was so slow that I was short of breath in the intervals. I didn't know anything about this man, he had no family around him, but at a time like that it didn't really matter, because eventually you're watching a soul and its body, yes ... from which the spirit is leaving. You can see it in the breathing. That left a deep impression on me.

It was a very special and peaceful experience. It wasn't frightening in the least to watch life leaving someone. The spirit, the soul or the breath was simply leaving. At one point his breathing was so irregular that I thought, isn't it strange that it's only afterwards that you realise it was someone's last breath, and not at the actual moment it happens. I decided to really concentrate and at a certain moment I thought; this is his last breath. And it was. You can feel it. In the intervals, you don't know whether or not there will be another one but I suddenly had the feeling: this is the last one. It was such a special experience. Then I thought: he is dead now, but for a moment I didn't do anything, I just sat there. It was so funny because after a couple of minutes, there was a sigh and his face seemed to relax a little. This happened again a few minutes later and his head fell to one side. It was as though his body was still letting go in stages.

DYING: A PRECIOUS AND ESSENTIAL PROCESS

That dying is not one single event, but rather a process that can be heralded by end-of-life experiences' (ELE) is self-evident once you acknowledge the experiences of hospice caregivers in palliative care as a possible reality. Although we cannot know what the dying person is going through inside, sensitive carers and relatives at the deathbed can recognise the highly personal and essential character of the process that the dying go through. ELEs also indicate that dying is a transition to another form of existence. A transition which does not have to be lonely or frightening, but something which is, to a great extent, full of hope, according to Fenwick. Fenwick's research has shown that not all those who are dying will experience ELEs. The frequency with which these phenomena occur, corresponds to the percentage of approximately ten percent that he and other scientists have put forward in respect to near-death experiences. We still do not know why one person has such experiences while others do not. There is also still a lot we don't know about consciousness. We therefore cannot make the conclusion that ELEs are a prerequisite for a good death. By extension, we also cannot conclude that hospice caregivers or carers who do not have these experiences might not be good carers. Nurse Loes is an excellent example of someone who provides good and loving care by being open to the needs and wishes of the dying entrusted to her care, without having these kinds of experiences. There are many others like her. Yet we have seen how essential it is to be receptive and sensitive to what more can happen around the deathbed. A good death doesn't have to be heralded by the phenomena described in this book, but recognising and accepting the phenomena and experiences of the dying, when they happen, definitely contribute to the care of the dying in the transition area of the death.

RELEASING A 'GOOD DEATH'

Is there such a thing as a good death? Who decides what is a good death and what isn't? Isn't a good death a highly personal matter? Some people cling to the belief that they can complete their lives in a good way by coming to terms with the lives as they were lived or by saying goodbye to all their loved ones. Others would prefer to go to bed one night and not wake up the next morning. There are also those who would like to have a painless death, to stay in control, or to maintain their dignity. Research has shown that people have different wishes and needs. Recognising these differences contributes to what many people would call a good death, as well as fulfilling the specific needs of the dying person in the final stages. Because that same research has shown that what actually happens is not always in accordance with the wishes of the dying, whether it is a wish to die at home surrounded by family and loved ones, or decisions about their treatment and pain medication. Talking about these needs and wishes beforehand, even if it's only around the kitchen table at home, contributes towards a better balance between needs and care. Accommodating these needs and wishes still doesn't say anything about a good death, while the non-fulfilment of these needs and wishes doesn't mean that it will not be a good death either. These needs and wishes, however relevant, that occur in this phase – the phase just before we see ourselves enter the irrevocable end of life – generally stem from our state of mind at the time. They have to do with our judgements and our thoughts and ideas about how it ought to be. They have to do with maintaining command, with control and management. There is nothing wrong with knowing what your own needs are, but be aware that it could turn out to be very different and that even your own worst thoughts and ideas could turn into reality. Just like any other phase in our lives, dying is much less of a controlled and managed process than we would like it to be. As long as we insist on trying to control how and when death will occur, we are unable to allow ourselves of being receptive to the unknown. The unknown that conceals itself in the veils of this transition, until we are able to face it. Time and again, I have seen that what is most essential about dying just cannot be directed by us. It is simply granted us, if we find ourselves in the flow of serving the autonomic process that dying entails. In order to do that we need to embrace the 'unknowing' and transcend the mental chatter that is our day-to-day consciousness.

We learn from the experiences of the hospice caregivers that in order to do that, we need to slow down and become calm. Becoming quiet inside ourselves makes us conscious of our own inner workings and dynamics. We learn to recognize our thoughts and assumptions concerning what is right and what isn't. We learn to shed a light on our beliefs, fears, and insecurities, so that we know what is part of our self and what is part of the other person. This brings us to our own inner knowing and to recognizing what the inner knowing is of the person dying and of those near and dear to him. We need to be silent and really listen, something we have heard from many of the hospice caregivers. Listening gives us access to a deeper understanding, to a deeper level of knowing.

Silence has become a scarce commodity in our society. We are constantly bombarded by noise and information from the outside world, which leads to a lot of mental noise and hustle and bustle. Meditation is one way to once again learn to listen consciously. Even having just a few minutes of silence every day can enable us to refine and deepen our ability to listen. In that silence we rediscover the connection to ourselves and from there the connection to others.

When we can let go of the idea of a good death because we realise that a good death comes from preconceived ideas, it gives us space. This is the space that hospice caregivers witness of when they talk about their role at the deathbed. It is an inner, spatial quietness, which gives testimony to complete availability and with which space is created for the dying. It is this space that allows the dying to connect with their own inner truths.

COMMUNICATING AT A
DIFFERENT LEVEL

There are many forms of suffering, but the most heartrending form of suffering is when we are unable to make a real and loving connection with others. Especially at meaningful moments and transitions in our lives. Dying arouses so many emotions. We shudder at the thought of having to say goodbye to our loved ones and so many of us have never learned how to deal with our emotions. Also our own unfinished emotional business plays its part when someone near to us is facing death. Because of our fears our hearts remain closed, so we cannot truly communicate with the dying, or make a real connection with them. And so we are unable to say or do those things which we know within ourselves are the right things. Despair and desolation are the result. Not only for the dying. Families and friends suffer when they have no idea what is happening, if decisions have to be made without knowing all the options, if they do not know or are unable to voice their own needs. Medical staff also suffer if treatments are started or reanimation is undertaken when they know deep down inside that these no longer serve the best interests of the dying. Whatever the individual needs and wishes might be, what applies to every one of us is that one wants to say what wants to be said, and one wants to do what needs to be done. Then there is rest and peace.

Whatever communication skills you have, talking about the approaching end seems for many to be a complex, emotional and time consuming exercise. The first step is understanding where, figuratively speaking, the other person is and joining him in his process. The person who is dying knows deep down that he or she is going to die. Relatives are also usually aware when the end is near. However, that knowledge, that truth is sometimes buried so deep and some people can't or won't face it. It's a matter of making aware what is already known inside. Being able to connect to the dying person's process and to explain what is happening, are important steps in guiding the dying and/or their relatives on their way to that truth.

Simone, supervisor:

> I was there when Patricia died and so was her brother. He had gone through a very unpleasant and traumatic experience with his own wife, who he had found dead. He just couldn't accept it and had stayed at home alone with his wife for several days afterwards. The doctor had to keep explaining to him that his wife was dead.

> Patricia was always the strong one. She was an intelligent lady of 50, and still had so many plans. It was very hard for her to let go. We tried to involve her brother and explained that it would be good for him to go through it with her. He still wanted to go to work, but during the final week he said he had finished anyway and spent a lot of time with us in the hospice. Patricia herself didn't have the feeling she was going to go, although it was obvious to us. She was so ill, she couldn't lie down anymore, she could only sit and we could see her becoming more translucent. She had said: 'I don't want to see my father, I feel so awful, he'll be coming after the weekend.' I told her: 'I don't think you will make it through the weekend. If you want to see your father, you should do it now.' Her father and brother duly arrived. They sat by her bed, but didn't know what to say. So I took charge a bit, explained what was happening, because no one really understood it.

> A day later it was indeed time. I had just popped in before I went home and I thought: she's going to die soon. I asked her brother if he would like me to stay with him, and he said: 'Yes, please', so I sat next to him and we waited together. She was sitting up in bed and was rather restless and was moving her hands a lot, but that's all she could do. I could see that there was a lot going on. She died quarter of an hour

later. I had to tell her brother what had happened four times, he just couldn't take it in. I had felt that it could bring him some healing but also knew that he couldn't do it alone. This is why I sat with him. It was very important for him to be part of it.

If we can help the dying to become aware of and possibly talk about what they know inside, then they will not miss the opportunity to relate to the reality. It's not uncommon for those involved to give a sigh of relief when that inner knowledge comes to light. Then the dying will be in a position to die their own good death. What we see hospice caregivers do, for example, is explain. Earlier, nurse Willy told us about explaining what happens in the process and how that brings comfort to the dying and especially to the loved ones.

Nurse Wilma, with twenty years' experience in terminal care, says:

> If someone is angry, I will say: 'I can see you're angry. It's alright to be angry, just let it all out'. I used to be scared of that anger. I thought they were angry with me. But no, it's all about the process they're going through.

Asking open questions can be a great help. What is most important to you? What do you think is happening now that you see your deceased mother? What do you think it is that's holding you here? Or as Josje asked: 'Why don't you choose where you would rather be?' In Josje's case this wasn't a problem, but we have to be very careful with why-questions. Some people can find why-questions too direct and might feel threatened. Even so, we shouldn't worry too much about these questions. The right questions also seem to come up naturally when the intention is to bring that inner knowledge, that truth, to light. That is communicating at a different level. After asking a question, it is important to be patient, to be quiet. It can take a while for the dying to be able to respond. We have to go along with the slowing pace of the dying. From that inner silence in which you then find yourself, it will not be a problem and there is no need to feel uncomfortable. The dying person needs time to find the answers within his or her inner self. It is also incredibly exhausting and even the slightest exertion is difficult.

Wilma:

Just listen and be there. I sit down, I listen, and sometimes I can explain things. I let people talk but I am also not afraid to ask questions. It's rare that a question doesn't hit the right spot. I try to follow my intuition. Certain things come to me and I have to absorb them. What should I do with this? Should I do anything at all? If that's the case then that's fine, but it is their process, I don't take over. I have to be a sounding board, to be there to listen, to just be there.

Some people who are dying really want to talk about their deaths but are not sure what to believe or think. They can ask questions such as: 'What do you think happens after we die?' or 'What do you believe in?' Sharing your thoughts can be very comforting and can help them to get in touch with their own beliefs. Sharing your own faith is not the same as evangelism. Evangelism is imposing one's own beliefs on someone else, but sharing your own beliefs is being open about what you believe in, while at the same time being prepared to listen to the other's point of view. If the dying ask you questions, answer them honestly, from your heart. Although it is good not to share personal matters, it can sometimes have its place. You have already read about volunteer Cok who told a religious resident that she reminded her of her grandmother who also believed, and how her grandmother was waiting for Jesus to come and collect her: 'That's what I told the lady and I could see her expression relaxing, and she was able to fall asleep.'

Sometimes the dying or their families literally need encouragement to say what needs to be said.

Jeannie:

I took a son in to see his father. He actually didn't dare to go in. His father was dying and that was very frightening for him. I said: 'Come on, we'll go in together.' We sat there together at his father's bedside. He was still conscious, so I said: 'Tell him that you're here, that you love him. Try to tell him those things that you still want to say.' So, that's what he did, and it was very moving. I'm sure that those last moments are extremely important. You take it with you on your onward journey through life, and if it's good, it can be very healing.

Sometimes the dying wait for permission to let go from their loved ones.
Volunteer Tini talks about a personal experience with her brother:

> My brother had already said goodbye to us, but it was actually my
> mother who told him: 'You can go now. It's okay. You did your best.'
> About an hour and a half later, he died. I had a strong feeling he had
> needed that permission, even though he was no longer communicating.
> It helped him to let go.

If said at the right moment, and if the intention is from the heart,
it can help the dying to let go when someone tells them that it's okay
to let go and that they have done their best. It's quite possible that the
dying either consciously or sub-consciously (?) consider their loved
ones' feelings and want to spare them. Sometimes the relationship is
so close that it seems impossible to let go. The following is a personal
experience of one of the volunteers, in which she tells of the extraordinary bond between those involved:

This is about my mother's youngest brother. He only felt at ease in
his own home when his wife, my aunt, was nearby. His wife was the
sort of person who liked to get things done. She was always in charge
and made all the decisions. He became more and more ill and was very
short of breath. On this particular day he was in their double bed, and
she lay beside him. She often did that, and put her head next to his. She
told us that she had no idea why she said what she did: 'Johan, I'm taking
you to a beautiful forest. You used to love that didn't you? Look at all
those different trees. Can you hear the birds?' My aunt could tell him
the names of all the birds. My uncle had always loved nature. She said:
'Just look, there's the light. Let's go towards it together. I can't leave the
forest, but you can. You can go on, it's allowed, and everything will be
alright. Go on, I'm here with you.' All the while he had lain there with
his eyes closed, but now he turned his head, looked into my aunt's eyes
and two thick tears rolled down his cheeks. Then he was gone. They
had actually travelled together to the threshold. My aunt is very down-
to-earth and it thoroughly surprised me when she told me.

If hospice caregivers or relatives are truly still and there is nothing that intervenes, then nothing really needs to be explained, said or
asked. This requires trust in and respect for the process as it comes to
pass. The inner, quiet space of the one who is near to the dying at that
moment reflects the deep understanding of the dying. You are the witness, and that is all that is needed to find profound meaning in death.

Lisette:

> We communicate on a different level. My father died here and I was
> very conscious of what happened and it was incredibly intense. My
> father was a man of few words. We did a lot with our eyes. He had
> also been very hard on himself and it was only in the last 24 hours that
> he allowed us to increase his medication against the pain. We gave
> him a morphine tablet which took effect within fifteen minutes. We
> were going to start using patches or a Dormicum pump the next day.
> They were all ready on his bedside table, but were never actually used.
>
> My father used to smoke. Suddenly he said: 'Have you got time to
> smoke a cigarette with me?' 'Yes' I replied, 'of course I have, and if you
> like, we can have another one as well.' He said: 'No, this will be the
> last.' I thought he meant that it would be the last for that day, but he
> never smoked again. He also said: 'I am going to the Eternal Light.'
> 'Okay. That sounds lovely', I told him. 'Yes', he replied. He didn't say
> much after that, but the expression in his eyes kept changing. It was
> a kind of wonderment as if he were asking himself: 'Where am I?'
> Then he looked straight at me, and I told him that I was still there. I
> held his hand tightly and then he asked: 'What's happening? I don't
> understand it.' I saw his eyes flicker. Meanwhile my mother, sister, her
> friend, and the two dogs had come into the room. He was lying on
> his side with his hands crossed over each other, resting on the side of
> the bed. Every so often he raised his eyes and looked at each one of
> us in turn. We nodded and he nodded back, and then he closed his
> eyes again. My father died in our midst saying goodbye consciously,
> yet without words. We communicated on a different level.

When the end is approaching and we have picked up all the signals,
such as a change in language and behaviour, possible ELEs, sudden
changes in the process, then we can be at peace with the knowledge
that those involved are aware of what is happening. The dying just need
a silent presence to gain access to it. Meditation, quiet moments or for
example the threshold exercise all help to calm your thoughts, be quiet in yourself and just be there for them. It gives the dying the space
to relate to the reality of that moment. This is how we can make our
unique contribution to the precious process of dying.

Even if you feel that you are unable to do this, then that's alright as
well. Knowing your own limitations is a brave thing to do. If you do

not want to talk about death with the dying person because it makes you uncomfortable, or if you feel that he or she doesn't want to talk to you about it, then it is probably better if someone else initiates the discussion. Trusting in the process of death, and respecting that this is the way it should be, also means that you do not have to force yourself. What matters is that you feel at ease, that you are quiet and are there for them. So if that is not the case, then just make sure that someone else is available and that you share your own uneasiness with someone if you need to.

SPIRITUAL CARE

In her book *Believe in life*, Myriam Steemers-van Winkoop suggests that there is no palliative care without spirituality. The definition of palliative care by the World Health Organization[17] with which professional carers work, includes not only the physical care but also the psychological, social and spiritual care. Each field deserves attention but, in this book, I limit myself, and then only summarily, to spiritual care.When death is in sight, writes Steemers-Van Winkoop, spirituality becomes important because it's at that time that people really begin to ask if death is the end, or if there is something beyond the threshold between life and death, and if God exists. Everyone tries to find the answers from the inner essence of their being. Spirituality refers to that essence. Religion can mean a great deal to some people but there are also those without religious backgrounds, such as non-church goers, humanists, atheists and agnostics, who have their own spirituality that answers their questions about existence.

Recognising and accepting the experiences and sensations of the dying in the transitional period of death is part of spiritual care. An

---

[17] Palliative care is an approach that improves the quality of life of patients and their families facing the problem associated with life-threatening illness, through the prevention and relief of suffering by means of early identification and impeccable assessment and treatment of pain and other problems, physical, psychological and spiritual (World Health Organization, 2002).

essential precondition for spiritual care is the acknowledgement of spirituality in one's own life. If we don't do that, we can all too easily miss the questions and experiences with which the dying might be struggling. Spiritual care must always be in harmony with the dying. It should never be the intention to impose one's own beliefs or traditions, or to force acts of faith upon another person. Praying or meditating with someone can provide comfort but must be done from the purest of intentions. Regular carrying out of familiar spiritual practices such as praying, reading from the Bible, or other religious texts, and performing a religious anointment, can give believers something to hold on to, encouragement, comfort, or inspiration during sickness and death. There must be a reason why the dying suddenly want to sing hymns or hear readings from the Bible. For those who believe in God, but do not follow any traditional religion, the power of prayer with inspired devotion, in their own words and straight from the heart, can be very meaningful. Buddhism has specific meditations for the moment of death, such as the Essential Phowa, the meditation of compassion and devotion and deep meditation to find rest in the very nature of the being. In the Jewish tradition, encouragement and hope are found in the positive deeds during life. Jewish tradition recognises the *Widduy*, a confessional prayer. The words of the Shema: *Shema Yisrael* will be spoken at the moment of death.

Offering support to the individual desires and specific questions of the dying is all part of spiritual care. Also for those who don't believe. But how do you provide spiritual care for someone with no faith? You can try to find out what that person's source of inspiration is, or what would give them hope. You can create a sacred atmosphere, and explore the meaning of the life lived together with the person who is dying, or help in not having to face death with empty hands and by concentrating on thoughts of high quality. These are characterised by love, harmony, beauty, truthfulness, purity, and peace. But amongst all of this, most important is to realize that non of us really knows what happens after death, that dying is a process that belongs to the dying themselves and that our role is only to bring to light what one knows deep down inside.

CONCLUSION

In this day and age, palliative care is on the public agenda and attention is being paid to the questions and choices in respect of (ongoing) treatment, pain management, palliative sedation and euthanasia. This is a great step forward. However, this book is not about such choices and in no way tries to pass judgement on choices that are made. Dying is a highly personal process that is determined by religious beliefs, spiritual convictions, personal experiences, and cultural background. Nor does this book try to romanticise death or to deny suffering. There is suffering, and death can be very distressing. All too often there is massive struggle at the deathbed and dying appears to be great turmoil for the loved ones too. Naturally, there is no intention to deny or cover up any feelings of grief after the loss of a loved one. You do not need to go through it alone, and if you do need guidance after losing someone who is dear, it's important to find a good grief counsellor near you.

What hospice caregivers can teach us is how we can develop our sensitivity in recognising and acknowledging these deathbed experiences and sightings. They teach us to be still and calm and to lend our own unique contributions when our loved ones are dying.

It might be that this book will encourage you to think more about your own approaching death. How will I die? How will I prepare myself? And in the mean time, how should I live? It could be that the experiences of the dying, their families and the hospice caregivers have brought about even more questions. Rather than being an ending point, this book could be the start of a process that progresses into a personal quest in which you can develop your own insights and interpretations about dying and death. I would like to invite you to take the time, and where possible, to stay in the not-knowing, or as Rainer Maria Rilke puts into words: "to be patient, to regard your questions with love and not to look for answers yet."

I dearly wish for the experiences in this book to serve as an inspiration, and I hope they bring you nothing but good on your path through life.

> Be patient toward all that is unsolved in your heart and try to love the questions themselves, like locked rooms and like books that are now written in a very foreign tongue. Do not now seek the answers, which cannot be given you because you would not be able to live them. And the point is, to live everything. Live the questions now. Perhaps you will then gradually, without noticing it, on some distant day, find the answer.[18]

---

[18] Rainer Maria Rilke (1875 - 1926), From: *Letters to a young poet.*

AFTERWORD

I neke Koedam has worked in Hospice *De Vier Vogels* in Rotterdam and other hospices, and her experience with the dying and her connection with so many other hospice staff and volunteers, who she has known personally and interviewed, has given her a special insight into and understanding of the mental state of the dying. This is reflected in her book, which shows clearly the outstanding care given to the dying by the hospice services in Rotterdam. In the course of my own research, I have spent some time talking to the staff of *De Vier Vogels* and quickly realised the extent of compassion, medical care and understanding shown by its staff.

We are now moving out of the phase where medical personnel consider the experiences of the dying to reflect pathology rather than having a meaning of their own. The frequency of these experiences means that we can no longer take this attitude towards them, or allow them to be ignored. Recent studies have shown that over 50% of patients who die consciously have the experiences Ineke describes. Equally interesting is the recent work which shows that over 50% of a group of patients dying of cancer had transcendent experiences in the days or hours just before death. These intensely spiritual experiences can be healing for both the dying and their carers, especially if they can be understood and discussed between them before the actual process of dying begins.

Ineke Koedam has a deep understanding of what it is like to die, and her focus is primarily on the emotional and spiritual needs of those who are dying and the way these can be met by those caring for them. This makes her book of inestimable value to us all.

Peter Fenwick, 2014

TRAINING AND
INFORMATION

Being a witness to the intimate process of dying is a privilege and respecting confidentiality is of the utmost importance. Yet these experiences can be very intense, and perhaps become a burden if you do not talk about them. It is important that you know you have support and that you can use it if ever needed. If you are a carer, make sure that you can go to one of your colleagues or supervisors. If you do have intense experiences in your own life, please make sure you can share your story with someone who you feel safe with.

Please feel free to share your own personal experiences via info@weerschijn.nl.

Together with Sue Brayne, Peter Fenwick wrote *Nearing the end of life, a guide for relatives and friends of the dying* and *End-of-life experiences, a guide for carers of the dying*. Both guides offer valuable instructions and can be downloaded free on <u>www.inekekoedam.com/research/</u>.

For lectures or training, please contact Ineke Koedam,Weerschijn at info@weerschijn.nl.

RECOMMENDED
LITERATURE

Brayne, Sue and Fenwick, Peter (2008). *End-of-life Experiences, A Guide for Carers of the Dying.* (GB)

Brayne, Sue and Fenwick, Peter (2008). *Nearing the End of Life, A Guide for Relatives and Friends of the Dying.* (GB)

Fenwick, Peter and Fenwick, Elizabeth (2008). *The Art of Dying.* Londen: Continuum.

Kübler-Ross, Elizabeth (1969). *On Death and Dying.* New York: Simon & Schuster/Touchstone.

Lommel, Pim van (2011). *Consciousness Beyond Life: The Science of Near Death Experience).* HarperOne.

Moody, Raymond (2001) Rider; 25Anniversary Ed edition

Rinpoche, Sogyal (1994). *The Tibetan Book of Life and Death.* Harper SanFrancisco.

Stafford Betty L. (2006). 'Are They Hallucinations Or Are They Real?' *Journal of Death and Dying,* 53, no. 1-2, 37-49. New York: Baywood Publishing Company.

ACKNOWLEDGEMENTS

First of all I would like to thank Dr Peter Fenwick, internationally renowned neuropsychiatrist, member of the British Royal College of Psychiatrists and an exceptionally sensitive and kind person. I would like to thank him for the trust he has shown in me when I embarked on his important study in the Netherlands. A study which could not have taken place without the willing and committed hospice caregivers from the three hospices which took part. My thanks to the 'De Vier Vogels' Hospice in Rotterdam, the Kajan Hospice in Hilversum and the Johannes Hospitium in Wilnis. I should also like to mention in no special order: Suzanne, Simone, Annelies, Jeannie, Lisette, Josje, Joke, Floortje, Gieneke, Gon, Anita, Ruth, Ina, Tina, Hilly, Cynthia, Winifred, Tjitske, Wilma, Loes, Loes H., Lyda, Tini, Helen, Anke, Cok, Liesbeth, Cocky, Diny, Willy and Mieke. I look back at the special, truthful meetings with each of them with a great feeling of gratitude and affectionate solidarity. I would also like to thank Christina and Esther for their generosity in sharing their moving personal experiences and allowing us to include these in this book.

My thanks also goes to my esteemed co-readers who, with their valuable feedback, contributed so much to the quality of the final result. Jeanine Mies of MIES/tekst & training for her professional, pleasant and expert feedback in the preliminary stages. Very special thanks to my father Cor Visser, for his unassuming and affectionate commitment to me and my work. His wish that this book would be available to many and be stocked by all GP practices because of its wealth of information and expertise makes me happy. My husband, Hans Koedam, for his crystal-clear criticism, which pushed me to realise my best potential. Mañec van der Lugt, originator of the symposium Endless Consciousness (2009) and who has been involved in Fenwick's work for a long time, for her sensitive review of my manuscript and apposite suggestions. Simone de Kuyper, hospice supervisor for her gracious wisdom and sense of nuance.

I am especially grateful to Pim van Lommel for agreeing to write the preface. From 1977 until 2003, Pim van Lommel was working as a cardiologist at the Rijnstate Ziekenhuis in Arnhem. Since then, he has given lectures all over the world about near-death experiences and the relationship between consciousness and brain function. Right from the start, I had the clear idea that he would write the preface. As the author of *Consciousness Beyond Life*, in which he explains his scientific vision about death experiences, he is often asked to write prefaces and to give advice. I was extremely pleased that he agreed to my request. As he says: 'An important book for everyone who works in a hospice and for terminal patients and their families.'

Finally, I would like to express my heartfelt thanks to Jon Beecher of White Crow Books. With his commitment and expert care, he made it possible for *In the Light of Death, Experiences on the Threshold Between Life and Death* to see the light in the English language throughout the world.

Paperbacks also available from
White Crow Books

Elsa Barker—*Letters from
a Living Dead Man*
ISBN 978-1-907355-83-7

Elsa Barker—*War Letters from
the Living Dead Man*
ISBN 978-1-907355-85-1

Elsa Barker—*Last Letters from
the Living Dead Man*
ISBN 978-1-907355-87-5

Richard Maurice Bucke—
Cosmic Consciousness
ISBN 978-1-907355-10-3

Arthur Conan Doyle—
The Edge of the Unknown
ISBN 978-1-907355-14-1

Arthur Conan Doyle—
The New Revelation
ISBN 978-1-907355-12-7

Arthur Conan Doyle—
The Vital Message
ISBN 978-1-907355-13-4

Arthur Conan Doyle with
Simon Parke—*Conversations
with Arthur Conan Doyle*
ISBN 978-1-907355-80-6

Meister Eckhart with Simon Parke—
Conversations with Meister Eckhart
ISBN 978-1-907355-18-9

D. D. Home—*Incidents in my Life Part 1*
ISBN 978-1-907355-15-8

Mme. Dunglas Home; edited,
with an Introduction, by Sir
Arthur Conan Doyle—*D. D.
Home: His Life and Mission*
ISBN 978-1-907355-16-5

Edward C. Randall—
Frontiers of the Afterlife
ISBN 978-1-907355-30-1

Rebecca Ruter Springer—
Intra Muros: My Dream of Heaven
ISBN 978-1-907355-11-0

Leo Tolstoy, edited by Simon
Parke—*Forbidden Words*
ISBN 978-1-907355-00-4

Leo Tolstoy—*A Confession*
ISBN 978-1-907355-24-0

Leo Tolstoy—*The Gospel in Brief*
ISBN 978-1-907355-22-6

Leo Tolstoy—*The Kingdom
of God is Within You*
ISBN 978-1-907355-27-1

Leo Tolstoy—*My Religion:
What I Believe*
ISBN 978-1-907355-23-3

Leo Tolstoy—*On Life*
ISBN 978-1-907355-91-2

Leo Tolstoy—*Twenty-three Tales*
ISBN 978-1-907355-29-5

Leo Tolstoy—*What is Religion
and other writings*
ISBN 978-1-907355-28-8

Leo Tolstoy—*Work While
Ye Have the Light*
ISBN 978-1-907355-26-4

Leo Tolstoy—*The Death of Ivan Ilyich*
ISBN 978-1-907661-10-5

Leo Tolstoy—*Resurrection*
ISBN 978-1-907661-09-9

Leo Tolstoy with Simon Parke—
Conversations with Tolstoy
ISBN 978-1-907355-25-7

Howard Williams with an Introduction
by Leo Tolstoy—*The Ethics of Diet:
An Anthology of Vegetarian Thought*
ISBN 978-1-907355-21-9

Vincent Van Gogh with Simon Parke—
Conversations with Van Gogh
ISBN 978-1-907355-95-0

Wolfgang Amadeus Mozart with Simon
Parke—*Conversations with Mozart*
ISBN 978-1-907661-38-9

Jesus of Nazareth with Simon Parke—
Conversations with Jesus of Nazareth
ISBN 978-1-907661-41-9

Thomas à Kempis with Simon
Parke—*The Imitation of Christ*
ISBN 978-1-907661-58-7

Julian of Norwich with Simon
Parke—*Revelations of Divine Love*
ISBN 978-1-907661-88-4

Allan Kardec—*The Spirits Book*
ISBN 978-1-907355-98-1

Allan Kardec—*The Book on Mediums*
ISBN 978-1-907661-75-4

Emanuel Swedenborg—*Heaven and Hell*
ISBN 978-1-907661-55-6

P.D. Ouspensky—*Tertium Organum:
The Third Canon of Thought*
ISBN 978-1-907661-47-1

Dwight Goddard—*A Buddhist Bible*
ISBN 978-1-907661-44-0

Michael Tymn—*The Afterlife Revealed*
ISBN 978-1-970661-90-7

Michael Tymn—*Transcending the
Titanic: Beyond Death's Door*
ISBN 978-1-908733-02-3

Guy L. Playfair—*If This Be Magic*
ISBN 978-1-907661-84-6

Guy L. Playfair—*The Flying Cow*
ISBN 978-1-907661-94-5

Guy L. Playfair —*This House is Haunted*
ISBN 978-1-907661-78-5

Carl Wickland, M.D.—
Thirty Years Among the Dead
ISBN 978-1-907661-72-3

John E. Mack—*Passport to the Cosmos*
ISBN 978-1-907661-81-5

Peter & Elizabeth Fenwick—
The Truth in the Light
ISBN 978-1-908733-08-5

Erlendur Haraldsson—
Modern Miracles
ISBN 978-1-908733-25-2

Erlendur Haraldsson—
At the Hour of Death
ISBN 978-1-908733-27-6

Erlendur Haraldsson—
The Departed Among the Living
ISBN 978-1-908733-29-0

Brian Inglis—*Science and Parascience*
ISBN 978-1-908733-18-4

Brian Inglis—*Natural and Supernatural:
A History of the Paranormal*
ISBN 978-1-908733-20-7

Ernest Holmes—*The Science of Mind*
ISBN 978-1-908733-10-8

Victor & Wendy Zammit —*A Lawyer
Presents the Evidence For the Afterlife*
ISBN 978-1-908733-22-1

Casper S. Yost—*Patience
Worth: A Psychic Mystery*
ISBN 978-1-908733-06-1

William Usborne Moore—
Glimpses of the Next State
ISBN 978-1-907661-01-3

William Usborne Moore—
The Voices
ISBN 978-1-908733-04-7

John W. White—
The Highest State of Consciousness
ISBN 978-1-908733-31-3

Stafford Betty—
The Imprisoned Splendor
ISBN 978-1-907661-98-3

Paul Pearsall, Ph.D. —
Super Joy
ISBN 978-1-908733-16-0

All titles available as eBooks, and selected titles available in Hardback and Audiobook formats from www.whitecrowbooks.com

Lightning Source UK Ltd.
Milton Keynes UK
UKOW02f1029150217
294460UK00004B/163/P

9 781910 121481